FROM HACKNEY TO HILL FARM: A TAPESTRY
THREE SCORE YEARS AND TEN

FROM HACKNEY TO HILL FARM:
A TAPESTRY
THREE SCORE YEARS AND TEN

Mary E Hartshorne

COUNTRY BOOKS

Published by: Country Books
Courtyard Cottage, Little Longstone, Bakewell, Derbyshire DE45 1NN England

ISBN 1 898941 07 6

British Library Cataloguing in Publication Data:
a catalogue record for this book is available from the British Library.

DEDICATION

This book is for my husband, Jim
and my grandsons
Mark, Richard, Seth and Peter
and my granddaughters
Ruth Mary, Laura, Lisa, Joanna, Catherine Alice and Rachel,
who in their enjoyment of life
remind me of the Alice and Mary in this story.

Design and production:
Dick Richardson, Country Books, Little Longstone, Derbyshire DE45 1NN

Printed in England by:
MFP Design & Print, Stretford, Manchester M32 0JT

Colour origination by:
GA Graphics, Stamford, Lincolnshire PE9 2RB

CHAPTER 1

A CHILD'S EYE VIEW OF A QUAKER FAMILY

LONDON TO BIRMINGHAM

My Mother worked in a small grocery shop in Hackney, east London. Within sight and sound of the river, the empty shop still stands. Surrounded by new buildings its days must be numbered.

I can imagine my Mother amongst the fresh fruit and provisions brought daily from Covent Garden, by horse and cart, not far away

It is not difficult to understand the worry of an unmarried mother of the early nineteen-twenties with little means of support and as far as I can determine, no one to whom she could turn for help. When her two baby daughters were born it was inevitable that she would have to part from them.

We took our Mother's name of Hayhaiens, unusual as it is, I have never been able to trace its origin. I can only think that someone in the course of registering us hesitated and stumbled over the letters until it became jumbled. Only those who have held their first born in their arms can imagine the anguish this mother must have felt at the thought of parting. My sister and I were taken to the nearby Dr. Barnado Home to spend the first eight months of our lives in shared clothes and impersonal cots. Few of these babies held briefly, loved and parted from, are willingly handed over to the authorities. Be it in the twenties or the more affluent days of the seventies. I have always held a fond regard for my parents knowing that all my qualities, good or bad, are an inheritance that no upbringing can completely erase or alter.

Being a twin is an interesting experience, although when young one is deprived of ever being alone, and often considered as half of a pair. 'The Twins', instead of a person in ones own right, there is always someone with whom to share the bath water. So it was that of all the children in the Home, at the age of eight months, Lucy and Elsie were chosen to become the adopted daughters of an elderly Quaker, William Littleboy, and his younger wife. In the arms or our new Mother and a nurse, Hilda, we travelled to Birmingham.

Edith and William with Mary and Alice, 1925

Lucy slept contentedly while I, Elsie, cried throughout the journey.

The Old House

"If you were to visit the old house you would find differences: the strip of field beyond the garden has now been built on and there is a footpath that runs along the other side of the garden fence where the clump of trees used to be. The garden is therefore much more overlooked than it used to be. There has been a lot of building going on towards Selly Oak, it is what you expect these days." So wrote my Uncle fifty years later than the day my twin sister and I were first tucked into our cots at South Hill. I have not been back to the house since I left it forty years ago, but the pictures of it in my mind are as clear as they were the day we left.

My Father, a retired business man, was in his seventies when he adopted us. One of the really good men of this world, he truly lived his religion in his everyday life. "That of God in every man" was never more believed, nor shown to be believed, than in the way he treated his fellow men. His family originally came from near Walford, where his father, Richard, was a miller. Later they moved to Newport Pagnell where he managed a Bank. At the mill Dad told me how he would run his hands through the grains of wheat and hear the steady swish of the grinding stones. The filling bags, the water race, and the smell of the meal meant home to him. He would climb the steps to the granary, his head close to his Father's boots. Too close, as he once told me, when he received a blow on the forehead never to be forgotten.

The boys of the family would throw sticks for the St. Bernard dog, who would jump off the bridge to retrieve them from the swirling river below. It was a happy family of three boys and a girl. William my father, and my Uncle Frank his brother who lived near us in Birmingham, and Aunt Anna were the ones I knew best.

After a time at boarding school in Scarborough, Dad had

worked in, and later owned, a brass industry in Birmingham. His Quaker teaching and writing earned him Wardenship of the Quaker College of Woodbrooke. After his retirement from industry he built his house, South Hill, only a fields distance away from the College. Here he lived with his first wife Margaret until her death. Dad eventually married again, an American wife, Edith. She was some years younger than he was, and my adopted Mother.

SOUTH HILL

Perhaps it was because South Hill had been a house without children for so long that it often seemed a frightening place to me. Facing south as its name implied and within sound and smell of the Cadbury's chocolate factory, the wind only had to be in our direction for the smell to drift up to us. The house, surrounded by trees to the west, could take on an eerie aura at night. I would lie in bed and listen to the owls; cats also seemed to abound and made the nights noisy with their cries.

I was four when, in our best clothes, we went to the Magistrates Court to have our adoption made legal. Although we had become Alice and Mary four years before, it was not until 1929 that the adoption order became law and a child could not be reclaimed at any time in his or her life by its natural parents. Playing in the back room of the Court, Alice and I were presented with a doll each. 'Peggy' as I called her, was dearly loved. One of my saddest days was when I learnt that 'she' had been thrown away — "her face was all worn out and you didn't want her any longer" I was told.

Of my Mother I remember little as she was to die shortly afterwards, leaving my father, then in his seventies, to cope with two lively daughters alone. I remember little of my Mother's kindness, or her personality which had so attracted my Father on one of his visits to America, eventually resulting in their marriage. Standing on the front steps I watched her getting into the taxi to take her to hospital. The greyness of the day is still with me. Alice and I stood side by side as the door closed on her. It was an illness from which she was not to recover. It must have been a strange irony that later she took her life in the Woodbrooke lake, a place that held many memories for my Father. A few sentences from a letter written by my Dad in June 1929 to Roger Clark, a 'Friend' shows his deep religious convictions and his beauty of writing. Talking of his wife's death he says "I can believe it was expedient for me that she went away: for it would have been terrible to see her suffer, and now although the outward blank sometimes seems insupportable I know she is at hand and can help me without the hindrance of physical infirmity. The last day of her life she was bright and cheerful and we walked about the garden and talked a great deal. But that evening she was greatly depressed: she told me she knew she would never get better. Had she lived a terrible operation of doubtful success was inevitable, and I am thankful that she has been saved from this. Our little girls — I had always thought of them as Edith's to cheer and comfort thro' long years after I was gone. Now all is changed, they are my great comfort, and I must try to live a little longer for their sakes. They are two of the sweetest children you ever saw. Surely in all these things, tho' they involve so much of sorrow there is the assurance that God, the author of love and beauty is in it all."

So it was that Beryl came to take charge of us. A Sister from St. Thomas' Hospital, in London, she quickly became 'Aunty' to us. Her brown eyes and auburn hair, making her vivacious character not easily forgotten.

My father wrote of her as 'dearly beloved daughter and Mother of my two little girls'.

Ten years later, when I was a student, invited to a friend's house for tea, I met Beryl's niece. Excepting the dark hair and that she was the same age as myself, here was the same Beryl in name and voice. I was taken back all the years to our house in Birmingham.

11

LIZZIE THE 'COOK OF COOKS'

Lizzie, our cook, ruled the household indoors as surely as Hall, the gardener, ruled the garden. Each morning Auntie Beryl would go through into the kitchen to discuss the menu, accepting Lizzie's decision on the day's meals as she in her turn would have to accept Hall's choice of vegetables from the garden. Lizzie was rosy-faced and grey haired, large and stone deaf. Talking to her was always carried on with some difficulty. One of our favourite games was to run down the stairs and across the kitchen, in front of the big coal range and out of the back door without having been seen. A thing of little difficulty if her back was turned to us while she was busy at the big scrubbed kitchen table! Lizzie could hug us to her starched and aproned bosom as easily as she could scold us. I well remember my Dad exclaiming in exasperation when yet again Lizzie had gone her own way in some matter "she's as deaf as a post." Once a year Lizzie went on holiday and the whole house took on a holiday atmosphere when Mrs. Mason and her son Edwin came to take over the running of South Hill. While Lizzie was at Weston-Super-Mare I would watch Edwin with his ball and his bicycle, longing to be invited to play!

Hall would dig the garden. In the Autumn he would bring in the apples and we would climb with Dad to the loft and lay them out in sweet-scented rows. Together it was an exciting place, but alone it could take on a haunted feeling of aloneness. The sloping roofs and the darkness due to the shrubbery outside threw shadows on the landing. The little bedrooms up there held all the promise of a much coveted room of one's own, but when the opportunity came fear soon got the better of me and I had to admit I preferred to be downstairs. We would pull out an old suitcase from under the bed and be allowed to hold my Mother's doll. Made of white kid, the china face, with shutting eyes, was framed by real hair. After a minute we had to return her to the safety of the tissue paper. How much better, I would think, if even at the risk of being broken she could have a proper home

Bournville village 1926

13

amongst the dolls in the nursery below.

Hall was a remote figure who would arrive each day to his work in the garden. It was only once that I glimpsed his life at home, or that I ever thought of him as having a home! Alice and I were taken to his terraced house in Northfield to visit his wife. Bed- ridden, she lay propped up by numbers of pillows. Such was her illness that she cried all the time. Standing beside the bed the horror of the scene took all words from me as I pulled towards the door. Crusty, Hall may have appeared to us but as he worked at a safe distance, I would watch a robin flit between turned earth, spade and barrow. He at least had one friend.

The central figure in our lives was, of course, Dad. The central room, the study. Here he would read to us every night, sitting on his knee we would ask for the book to go on for ever. When we were young, it would be all the simplest tales. Later the classics, 'At the Back of the North Wind', 'A Hundred Leagues under the Sea', he never sat down after tea without some book he had chosen to start on. When I was older I would sit at the table doing my homework. The pictures above the fireplace of "The Praying Hands" and "The Light of the World" as clear to me now as the coloured matches with which we would light the fire after dinner. "What does it mean in the picture?" I would ask "to stand at the door and knock and Christ will open it unto you".

Bed time would come and up the wide staircase we would have to go. When I was young I often regretted the fact that at school the other children had the wireless and lived a much more modern life than we did. None of the ritual of morning readings from the Bible, prayers at night for them. As we lay in our beds Dad would sit in the hall below winding his gramophone. He would open the two doors at the front and the music would fill the house. What other child can look back with nostalgia to bed time when they hear the pastoral symphony or Strauss waltzes as we did. Our teeth cleaning was accompanied to 'The Tales from the Vienna Woods'. It didn't make me musical, but I learnt early of the joy or being able to sink into a world of the imagination while the music went on around me.

The Garden

Although we were brought up in the ordered town house of a Quaker family it was in the realms of the garden that I first got my taste for the country and country ways. Here the trees shed their acorns and their horse chestnuts. We could kick up the leaves ankle deep, to find the smooth red-brown nuts. Our chestnuts lay in the shoe boxes to go mouldy, the same as did the chestnuts of my own children.

From the garden there was very little in those days to remind one of the town. The field rose behind the house to block out all other houses. Except for the distant hum of traffic on the Bristol road on a summer night, one was far away from the activities of a town. I well remember a Waxwing taking up residence in the plane tree by the gate and the steady stream of visitors to see it. Tits and robins were numerous and rooks nested in the oak trees at the bottom of the garden. Dad loved the country and for this reason we were encouraged to know and name birds and plants.

When it was warm we were allowed to sleep out on the verandah. As the velvet still of the summer night changed to dawn hedgehogs would leave their tracks in the dewy grass in the same way as they do today in the deepest country. The smell of new mown grass came as sweetly on the wind as does that of new mown hay today.

The first introduction to biology that I can remember was painstakingly doing my 'nature' homework on the study table. No parent was more helpful or more proud than mine. His work received a regular A. My reward was an interest in country things that has lasted all my life.

I have lain in bed on many summer nights since I lived at South Hill, watching the evening darken. Over the gentle rolling hills of the West Country or the tall buildings of the town where the swifts shriek and wheel against the rosy light of setting sun and grey chimneys. Never more beautiful than the evening garden at South Hill where the lengthening shadows of the oak tree spread across the lawn and the sound or subdued voices rose to the open window. My Dad and Uncle Frank would cross and re-cross the lawn in an evening game or croquet. The gentle thud of the balls, wood against wood, music to my ears. Here full length under the slightly fading paint of the window sill I first watched a thunder storm roll up from the Welsh mountains across the great industrial plain of the Midlands. In the Pennines, where I now live, a storm suddenly springs upon you unawares from behind the hills and a clap of thunder can be almost overhead before you know it. Recently I was reminded of a Midland storm. Lightning will flicker and sheet so far off that no sound is heard. Gradually it comes nearer and the great expanse of sky shadows and reshadows the lightning until a rush of wind brings the rain and the noise of the storm. Only then did a sudden fear overtake me; from watching the beauty of the storm, I lay down in the warmth of my bed. I hear again my Dad approaching along the passage, to tell me not to hold the metal window catch in case I be struck by lightning as was a friend of his. "What happened then?" I wanted to know. "Was she dead?" "Yes she was quite dead and she fell to the floor".

I wrote of the garden the following poem, which even now I think I would have difficulty to better.

> When you lie in the open air
> and the wind plays with your hair,
> the sky is blue,
> the world seems new
> when you lie still.

How better could a summer day be described in the garden at South Hill.

THE DINING ROOM

The dining room was a sombre room in browns. Two large pictures of the Madonna and child hung on the walls. The bay windows overlooked the drive, where a weeping willow tree alternately hid us when we played in the summer, or shook its leaves in the wind and rain or winter. My father's leather bound books lined one or the walls, and the gas fire gently hissed when it felt cold enough for it to be lighted. One door opened onto the hall, the other to the pantry: behind this second door the sound of drawers opening and shutting, and the clatter of crockery being put away, was as much a part of the vacated dining-room as was the faint aroma of dinner recently cleared away.

Every morning after breakfast Dad would turn his chair to the fire, and opening his Bible prepare for the morning's 'Bible reading'. Lizzie and the maid Catherine would be summoned from behind the green baize door to take up their places on the chairs set out for them. My Father's voice would read whatever verses he had chosen for the day. Occasionally Alice or I would sit on his knee and read a verse, out loud, with him. I never remember a day when Dad did not follow the Quaker custom of Bible reading, participated in by all the family. Quakers from the earliest days had taken out the family Bible, and gathered, for just such a reading, in numerous homes in many countries in past years. By 1930, we were perhaps one of the few still to do so. What significance this has today is hard to guess at but I know that it gave us a great feeling of overcoming life's difficulties together, and a striving towards a common goal of 'right', that perhaps is lost in the busy hurry of the nineties. For what hurried breakfast of today, has the time or inclination to think much about the troubles of others? So busy are we with our own. The beautiful language of the Bible stories and the Psalms lodged in my mind, if not on the tip or the tongue, they were for ever recognised and loved. No Moffat translation, or New English Bible could ever sound the same, however more correct the meaning for today.

Here, also, Alice and I sat down alone for our high tea. At one corner of the table our plates were laid. Three pieces of brown bread and butter, the first without jam, and a glass of milk. Sitting opposite Alice, the claustrophobic atmosphere of good behaviour sometimes became impossible to endure. I remember dissolving into giggles of spluttered milk and crumbs until I slid from my chair to the floor in uncontrollable laughter. No one can have sat with their children at tea, not to have had the experience of this. Some chance remark that set off a crumby explosion, bringing laughter to all the family. My husband, once coming upon such a scene, remarked, "Do you really allow them to behave like this?" For who, not having experienced 'Dining-room tea' could understand the memories evoked in this helplessly giggling mother?

It was to the dining-room, that came a cook to be interviewed for a job at South Hill. Why this was so I cannot now imagine. It would have been impossible to replace Lizzie, or to have given her an understudy. Several minutes lapsed with Aunty Beryl and the cook behind closed doors. Alice and I waited with interest in the hall. Eventually, a strange little becoated figure emerged to shamble out of the front door, down the steps and up Oak Tree Lane towards the station.

A Baker's Dozen

A summer evening and a love of being outside led Alice and me to one or our most remembered evenings. Behind the house the baker turned out his horses to graze at night. After the day pulling the baker's carts from house to house the huge bay and grey horses stood under the shade of the trees in the field lazily flicking their tails at the flies. They would lean over the fence to be stroked by anyone who cared to do so.

Our playmate Rachel and her young brother, Bunny, as he was then called, went over the fields to see the horses. Rachel lived in the grounds of Woodbrooke College. Her father, Jack Hoyland, a tall figure with his deep voice, was known to all Quakers of that time. A champion of the unemployed — his opinions not always met with acceptance. One or Rachel's elder brothers had lost his life on a Swiss mountain, her uncle, his on Everest. Ironically, fifty years to the day of my writing this, the attempts are still being made to climb the more difficult routes and men are still losing their lives on the mountain. This evening with Bunny firmly held

William Littleboy with Mary and Alice, 1932

by the hand we soon tired of trying to round up a Shetland pony in the next field, and we turned our attention to the horses leaning over the gate. It was suggested, I do not know by whom, that we should climb from the gate onto their backs. Our riding went well, and it was lucky that we did not fall off, with their huge feathered feet stamping below.

All went well until, leaning over the gate, Bunny triggered off some jealousy in another of the horses. Savagely he was bitten across the face. The screams could have been heard far away and appaled at what we were unwittingly responsible for, we hurried Bunny home. Alice and I were not met with pleasure on the door step. We looked guilty, were presumed responsible and were sent home. Fearing the worst in the form of punishment we said nothing. Several days later I denied that there was any reason for our quietness. When I asked if we would be able to play with Rachel, I got the surprising answer that we were not to play with her again. As we received no punishment ourselves, I guessed we were not the only ones who thought it a little unreasonable. I did not meet Rachel until a number of years later, when she came to the same boarding school as I was at. I walked towards her down the drab, linoed corridor, to ask her if she remembered that summer evening. Not one look of recognition passed between us. The moment for speech had passed as moments for speech often do. Silence held me and although I was to see her every day for several years, so strong was the power of the adult world over us that I never spoke to her once.

Fifteen years later when my youngest son was born I received a post card of congratulation from Jack Hoyland. Perhaps we had not been in such disgrace as I had thought.

LITTLE GIRL LOST

Alice was always the leader, the spokesman, and mostly I was happy for this to be so. She was the oldest and the tallest and I believe, the sweetest. So wrote my Dad in one of his letters which I still have, "Alice is a sweet child" and I smile now to think of him; did he leave any mention of Mary because he did not quite know what to say about her? I was more timid than Alice and being good and sensible did not come to me easily in that big house. Many hours passed solitarily behind the locked door of my bedroom, awaiting me to say I was sorry and would try and do better next time. To be fair to Dad, I believe many a time of our being confined to our bedrooms, he, too, remained uninterfering in the study below, with difficulty.

This particular afternoon we were playing in the garden when Alice disappeared. We looked everywhere and she could not be found. Several hours went by and then the Police were informed. I was asked if I knew where she was. My answer of "no", but that I knew she would soon return, was not due to some twinnish telepathy. Like the proverbial bad penny I was sure she would turn up. Throwing all worry to the wind I made the very best of the afternoon. All the toys Alice would normally have had the first turn on or the longest time with, were mine for the taking. Never had a small girl enjoyed being the only child so much. Sure enough, Alice did return, as dusk began to fall she came in through the gate on her bicycle with a daisy chain round her neck and cakes in a serviette. Hilda, who had helped my Mother bring us home from the orphanage had taken Alice home for tea. Poor Hilda, unable to have children of her own, had adopted a little boy. She being quite unable to look after him the authorities had taken him back, so she thought she would borrow a child for the afternoon. Little did she know the alarm she had caused. I scorned the daisy chain and refused to eat any of the cakes that Alice brought, but I was pleased to see her home.

High Days and Holidays

Sundays were of course High days and as such we had to exchange the reading of our usual story books for Bible stories and The Pilgrim's Progress. On Sundays, the drawing room fire was lit and it was tea with white bread and butter and apricot jam, with the grownups, instead of brown bread and butter alone in the dining room. We sat in the bay window, overlooking the garden. Sunday was Quaker Meeting day. When we were younger we went with Aunty Beryl to Northfield Meeting, the journey into Birmingham being considered too far. The bare dusty meeting left little impression of pleasure on me. The benches were hard, and the criss-cross of fading green lights above were there only to be counted. I think I am the only person to have swung their legs back and forward for the whole of the time we were in meeting. I was gently admonished for this by a Quaker lady afterwards. When it was thought that we were old enough we went to meeting with Dad to Bull Street Meeting in the centre of Birmingham. Here the seats were covered with blue cushions and although pushed between towering old buildings, giving it a curiously surrounded feeling, it was the New Bull Street meeting house. "God does not dwell in buildings, but in the hearts and minds of men", the words of George Fox did not seem quite so apt here as they had at Northfield. We would walk to the top of Oak Tree Lane and take a short cut to the tram which clanged and sparked its way into the centre of the town. On the older trams the whole of the top deck was open, the newer ones had open ends where one could watch the town slip by with the wind in your hair. The walk from the tram to meeting was through back streets and snickets, past small shops deserted on a quiet Sunday morning. Every street had a public house and the smell of the stale beer as we passed their washed steps was as much a part of Sunday as the trams or Sunday clothes.

There were a number of individualistic Friends attending Meeting then. As today the Society was full of people who thought for themselves and having thought, acted upon it. 'Women's Lib' has been in existence since the earliest Friends. It always seems a curious idea to me that 'Women' should not be equal to men. We were brought up to think that they had a place of importance in life. As Friends say "All men (and women) are equal in the sight of God".

My Father sat up in the front benches, being an elder of the Meeting. To the right of him sat the tall figure of Joseph Southall. He always wore his hat in Meeting. Occasionally Dad would gently try to bring a halt to a speaker who kept talking too long. Often he would stand up and, directing his gaze towards the children of the Meeting, would talk with a message we could understand. Looking round the silent bowed heads I would hope that Dad would speak. At last the shake of hands between the elders of the Meeting would bring it to an end and we would be on our way home again to Sunday dinner.

My earliest holiday away from home was one taken alone with Aunty Beryl. We were to visit her sister and husband in Margate. They owned a fish shop in the main street, with a flat above. The expedition at once took on excitement when I overheard it said that "he was no good". Later, standing in the door of his shop a friendly man in a blue striped apron spoke to us. Turning, slicing and slamming the white fish down on the counter I knew at once the grown ups I had overheard were wrong. Tea in the flat above with the little kitchen next door and the bedrooms along a short passage was very different from the rambling rooms at home. The warmth of the little home has stayed in my memory ever since.

One of our yearly outings always took place in the spring at South Hill. Aunt Anna, then in her seventies, would arrive from London and again by tram we would go to the terminus at the Lickey Woods on the outskirts of Birmingham below the Malvern Hills. Here the woods would be a carpet of bluebells, the paths stretching for miles with the distant Welsh mountains rising in the distance. The afternoon ended at a little wooden bridge and a cafe where hot buttered toast was ordered. Try how I may, I have never been able to equal the taste of that toast.

Aunt Anna was a rather forbidding lady. She did not seem to have a way with children and yet we loved her. All her commands would end with the word "child" which we took as an endearment rather than a reprimand. Even after many visits I always felt rather in awe of her.

Aunt Anna lived in Highgate, London, in a small house with

On William Littleboy's 80th birthday. (From left to right.)
Back row: Winifred Littleboy, Frank Littleboy, Anna Littleboy,
Slightly forward: Wilfrid Littleboy, (behind Anna), Harrison Borrow (clasped hands, next Ethel in white blouse).
Front row: Beryl Ashford, Mary Littleboy, William Littleboy (Dad), Alice Littleboy (standing), Nancy Miall (Nan), Grace Miall (Auntie Grace).

her servant and friend Vinah. Such a relationship of devotion and service is truly a thing of the past. Together they refused to leave Highgate throughout the 1939 war and under the kitchen table miraculously came through night after night of bombing and direct hits on nearby property.

When we were old enough we would visit her there and together on the top of the buses she took us to every part of London. She knew her city inside out. We went to Greenwich Observatory, the museums, Tower, Parks and Palace gates. Her knowledge of London was amazing and her fearless dashes across roads legendary. Born in an age before the era of cars she seemed completely to disregard their presence in her streets. Home again in the little three bedroomed house, Vinah would serve tea out of the silver teapot. A great talker, Vinah would finally close the door on Miss Anna to take her own tea in the little kitchen. I have often thought of these two remarkable ladies since. Vinah with all her friends and relations round about, whose doings she would relate to Miss Anna exuberantly when she came home from her afternoons off. Aunt Anna listening as to an amusing child.

Never were two people more different in character but equal in devotion for each other. I know little about Aunt Anna's early life, or her work, except that it was often among young people in Quaker settlements in London. As she was ten years younger than my Father she lived a number of years after him. A new side to her character was shown to me when my eldest son was born. She sent a pair of blue and white bootees. 'A special pattern that cannot be kicked off', she wrote. This was an Aunt Anna that I had never known, a more motherly person, knitting in her little sitting room with her books around her.

COUSINS

Near us in Birmingham lived our cousins Margaret and Christopher and their father and mother, Wilfrid and Winifred. Christopher was then only a baby and Margaret several years older than we were. We did not see much of them and I can never remember just going in our old clothes to play. Their visits to us were mainly at Christmas when we were in our best clothes.

My Uncle was a pacifist in the 1914 war and went to prison for his beliefs. Dad was already too old to be called up for the army in 1914. We took it for granted that war was wrong, as did our elders. Even though it was said that this was a 'war to end wars' (as though giving sense to it) Quakers believe in peace at all costs. To show the success of pacifism, the classic tale of the Indians in Pennsylvania is told. The Indians came to attack the Quaker settlers whilst they were in meeting. The fact that they sat on unafraid and did not fight back, so winning the Indians' friendship, being proof of the power of non-violence. We would always be asked "What would you do if your children were attacked?" as of course one would probably pick up the nearest weapon and defend them, it was an impossible question to answer to any sense. I wholeheartedly thought that my Father was right, but sometimes felt I would prefer to be like the other children around me. To have a Father who had fought in the war and go to Church instead of Meeting might make life easier. It was surprising how little was known about Quakers then, as today. We were still expected to wear grey bonnets and have no fun, as did the Quakers of 100 years ago.

All our family were clever. Dad told me that he only had to read through a page to remember it word for word. He also wrote a good deal and encouraged us to do so. He was a good and interesting speaker at evening meetings around Birmingham. It was one of these occasions when he had forgotten he was to attend an outlying meeting, the only time that I saw him flustered. Then in his late seventies the buttoning of his leather gaiters, having twelve buttons on each side, proved too much. My younger fingers speedily took charge. The incident sticks in my memory as the first time I realised that I might be useful in my own right.

I was proud and fond of my cousins but even at that early age I felt that I was 'with them and not of them' in the matter of outgoing personality and intelligence. Perhaps to some extent all adopted children feel this, and some other ones. Although it is generally possible to find some accounting for trait if ones family is known. Great Uncle George may have been the thief of the family, or little Aunt Julia the Bohemian. I followed Margaret to boarding school. Christopher also eventually went away to school in the same town.

Ten years after I had left Birmingham a strange thing happened — a coincidence to bridge the gap of years. It took place on a cold sleeting Saturday when I asked permission to visit the nearby 'Brick Ponds', a derelict workings tucked in beside the railway line and a housing estate. For some reason we were never allowed to go on walks on a Saturday afternoon. My teacher was so taken aback at the request that permission was given. Earlier in the week I had noticed a Whooper Swan amongst the two Mute Swans on the ponds, and I wanted to see again this beautiful bird with the reversed markings of yellow and black on its bill. A winter visitor to Britain they have a wildness and freedom about them that the semi-domesticated Mute is without. Standing on the cinder path watching the birds, stood a slight figure in a blue cap. "Are you Christopher?"I asked. I was not quite sure that this was my cousin as I had seen him so little since he sat in the high chair at South Hill for Christmas tea. With a common upbringing to appreciate birds, what chance had brought us to watch swans on the same cold Saturday afternoon, to bring back memories of South Hill days?

A Short History of the Quakers

In the nineteen twenties and thirties, when Alice and I were living in the Quaker family at Birmingham that I have described in these pages, Quakers were apt to be thought a little 'peculiar' as, indeed, they still are today. Without knowing much about their history, we were dismissed as 'those people who held meetings where no one preached! people who believed in dull clothes and

Jordans Meeting House and burial ground
Photographs taken from 'Jordans' by A. L. Littleboy "Aunt Emma" written in 1927

Interior of Jordans Meeting House. Showing bedroom through the open shutter

no music or fun.' So far from the truth is this that I am now going to outline a very brief history of the rise of Quakerism, and its ideals, so that no one reading this story can continue in being misled.

In the seventeenth century there began to be a number of people who could find no satisfaction in the religion of the day. It was a Puritan religion, which stressed the absolute infallibility of the word of the Church and Bible. This marked the great failure of the Reformation, in that the Church was 'losing its life' by demanding a religion built on terror and the fear of everlasting torment if it should be disobeyed. Increasingly, it seemed to be that the Church spoke of a Christ who had died for the few alone. There were few who, by better circumstances, were able to live by the word of the Bible, compared to the majority who were living humble and ordinary lives. It was a doctrine of despair for most and of false security for the few and quite incompatible with a faith in a 'Loving God'. The result was that in the 17th century people who found no satisfaction in this regime started to 'Seek out' a new religion, these were termed 'The Seekers'. "They waited in prayer, having no determination of things, nor any infallible interpretation of scripture". They were looking for a leader, or an 'Apostle' to give visible evidence of having come to lead them.

When George Fox began to preach, they thought they had found their 'Apostle'. He convinced them they had found what they were 'Seeking'. He preached God and Christ as one and the same. It was in fact, a return to the primitive Christianity, in that people were to leave the terrors of the dogma of the Puritan Religion, to have a direct relationship with a God who, through Christ, had lived a 'Divine life here among men'. So, as in the early Church this ever-loving God was to lead the people forth in 'a perilous adventure' for the redemption of the world. It is hard to see why such a harmless doctrine should receive such opposition. There were of course, many saintly Christians in the Anglican and Roman Church. The difference was that Fox was prepared to base his whole Church policy upon the 'Spirit's' presence and guidance, so sweeping away all the outward signs which the church had safe guarding its unity. For example an ordained ministry, set forms of worship, the sacraments and baptism, were, the Quakers said, no longer needed. With one voice therefore the Quakers were condemned as 'Heretics'; their doctrine seemed to foretell utter disintegration.

Somehow, Fox was able to shape a character in those who followed him which, for independence, truthfulness and courage, of Christian endeavour. From all the 'lsms' of the time, known as 'Ranters', with wisdom and patience Fox and his friends managed to prevent the doctrine of 'The Children of Light' from being wrecked. So it was that the Quaker movement went ahead unimpeded.

The greatest charge brought against the early Quakers was their belief of 'That of Christ in every man' so making salutation needless. They would not call the Bible the word of God, because, they said, 'The Divine Spirit' spoke direct to the hearts of man. The speaking was not some supernatural manifestation, but an ordinary language of the day. A reasoning and conscience that ought to influence a decision. From the 'Peculiarities of the Quakers' evolve the throwing aside of leaders and all set forms of worship. They met together in silence; anyone could, if led by the "still, small voice of God" pray or speak. There was no set service, no priesthood, no altar.

It was felt that since Christ himself was the leader, they must wait in silence for him to direct them. An arranged service denied liberty in the spirit of God and might easily be unreal. Silence, in the Quaker ideal of worship, is therefore not an end, but a means to an end! To meet in silence can to some seem a terrifying strain! Instead of forgetting oneself in hymns and the outward beauties of the Church, one is thrown back on oneself in a way they can hardly bear. The very best meeting, however, can communicate through silence. The people bring with them a help for each other. In the depth of the subconscious being, personalities blend together and influence each other. The point of the Quaker belief is that they know that "right doing" or "God's light" can be arrived at together and is not dependent on the, perhaps, distorted view of one preacher. Singing was also put on the same basis, leaving it open for the congregation to do what it felt best. In this 'Being led by The Spirit' women have, since the earliest time of Quakerism, been held equal to men before God. So, able to lead a meeting in speech or prayer.

In business, Quakers strove to be honest, and to live up to their principles. Later it brought them prosperity, which in some measure also brought a decline in their zeal. They would not bow or use flattering words, "Friends could not put off their hats or say 'You' to a single person, but 'Thou' and 'Thee'". People began to say "They will take the trade of the nation out of our hands!" It was the same feeling of equal worth of ALL men in the divine 'Spirit', that made Friends refuse to make the distinction between people; "You" was regarded as the address used only to a superior. "Thou" was used to equals. It was the same reason which led them to keep on their hats, even in the presence of judges and magistrates, a practice which caused them severe suffering. The removal of the hat should be reserved for God alone. The retention of the hat in places of Worship, except during vocal prayer, was regarded as a testimony against the false idea that one place could be in itself more Holy than another. This was the reason for the wearing of his hat by Joseph Southall, in our Meeting at Bull Street. A complete thing of the past today.

The plainness of dress, often a uniform grey, started as a protest against the spending of large amounts of money on dyes and ribbons. It was to try and express the true value of clothes and luxury. There was no active ruling against anything of beauty comfort or recreation. By 1911, Friends were left to consult their own conscience about such things. None of the testimonies of the early Friends brought more suffering than a refusal to take oaths in a court of justice. The penalty for refusing was forfeiture of all property, or outlawry. The Sermon on the Mount states 'Swear not at all' but it was said that without swearing in court, few would tell the truth. This implied a low standard of truthfulness to the Quaker, and was not acceptable. Any suffering was consid-

Left: *Hardwick House Farm. The new roof 1991.*

'In the spring the bats flew out completely undisturbed and the roof looked marvellous.'

Below: *Hardwick House Farm 1996.*

Right: *Mary with her eldest son, Kenneth, and grabdchildren Ruth, Laura and Peter.*

Below: *Jim with Catherine 1989.*

ered better than being thought a liar. By 1689, however, the Toleration Act gave Friends permission to 'Affirm' instead of swearing, their allegiance to the King; a few years later this also applied to courts. After 1888 it was permitted to make a solemn affirmation of intention to speak the truth.

The dilemma of the Testimony for Peace is also seen throughout history. In the early Christian Church, during the second and third centuries it was held, at least by its leaders, that Christians could not take part in wars. Reading our history books, one is apt to overlook this. The same view was held in the Middle Ages, so the emergence of the same conviction by Quakers was no accident. In 1651 George Fox was offered a captaincy in the army, and refused. I told them, it is said, 'I knew from whence it all arose, even from lust, according to James' doctrine and that I lived in the virtue of that life and power that took away the occasion of all wars'. Later, he was imprisoned for refusing to be a soldier. Gradually, the 'light' led some Quakers to follow suit. Although some felt it was right to defend themselves against invasion or to make use of the sword to suppress evil-doers, Quakers were left to decide their own course of action. In 1660, however, Fox made a declaration to Charles II: "We utterly deny all outward weapons, for any end or under any pretence whatsoever". "This is our testimony to the whole world". Friends of today do not hold identical views, but peace is still held as an ideal. It is often supposed that the Friends' belief of peace is founded on the interpretation of the Testament 'Love your enemies, resist not him that do evil.' Inevitably the inconsistency of taking these words literally and such commands to baptise or take the Sacraments not, was soon raised. This was however mainly done because the ordinary people could understand the word of the Scripture, whereas the vague answer of the Quaker Testimony being based on the 'Inward light' was not understood at all, and regarded as blasphemous heresy. It was a feeling that they were reproducing in their lives the spirit of a way of life, taken up by Jesus of Nazareth. Gentleness achieved a victory that force could never win. 'The light' could be seen in all mankind, of whatever creed, which they hoped would unite the world. How much this ideal, or how little has been achieved three centuries later, is a sobering thought. Quakers of this early time, and of the time I write, thought that the Testimony for peace was a unique contribution, if we had the courage to make it, in seeking the good in all men, and refusing to treat any as enemies. Perhaps it was an ideal that shows little relevance today, as man heads steadily towards his own self destruction. After the Great War of 1914, there was a great sense of hope and rebuilding. The League of Nation's agreed to disarm all nations and settle disputes in a judicial way. It was still a great possibility. The war of 1939 had not become a reality. It was perhaps one of the hopeful times for the peace of mankind. Many Quakers became Liberals, and worked for reforms in all the social fields of life, schools, hospitals and housing. There was a great sense of purpose, things could be achieved. Today, alas, although "Friends" and others still work, we seem almost to know that the cause for Mankind is hopeless.

Yet, to me, at any rate, the ideals of the early Quakers still seem to be founded on sound common sense, that all could do well to heed, whatever their religion, or lack of it, if they truly wish the world to survive as we know it.

SCHOOL AND WORDS. WORDS. WORDS

Words were of great importance to Dad. even though he would not have the new fangled wireless in his house.

At the age of five, Alice and I were sent to a private kindergarten school at Northfield not far away. I graduated from tying bows to reading but it was hard work. I was kept in after school until I could spell the word MOUNTAIN, the more flustered I became the more impossible the repeating of the right letters became. Defiant instead of my usual tears I was at last told to go. My teacher must have seen it was hopeless. In the

34

succeeding months I did teach myself. Of all the words I cannot spell today, MOUNTAIN is not one of them. At first we went to school by taxi, but later by bicycle. The roads divided below Bournville park. One was less built up than the other and had a spacious feeling of rising up over the hills. I usually took this one. At the dividing point a small house sticks in my mind as the ideal home where a child could live with a Mother and Father of their own. I found the Beech tree at the end of the park far more interesting than school. Flinging my bike down in the road I would walk about through the carpet of beech mast, cracking open the golden brown kernels to eat the milk-white nuts inside. Recently I tried to do the same under some Northern trees. The nuts were shrivelled and there were hardly any kernels.

At this time we often had students living with us from Woodbrooke College to learn English. Rigmor, a Danish girl, was with us for over a year. With her came a new interest into our lives. She would take us in turns on the carrier of her bicycle. Crossing the Bristol road, feet dangling dangerously near the wheels, the smell of the baked summer fields and the feeling of freedom as the wind rushed by is still with me.

One Sunday morning about this time, we climbed into bed with Aunty Beryl, one on each side of her as usual. We lay quietly, Dad came to tell us she was ill. A very few days later I awoke at night on a little camp bed in the nursery. Something felt wrong; the house was silent and all the lights were on, yet it was the middle of the night. I must have called out, for Rigmor was beside me. Smoothing my hair back from my forehead she murmured, "Poor child, poor child". In the morning I learned that Aunty Beryl was dead. Increasingly lost, as I suppose I became with a succession of students trying to take Aunty Beryl's place, the more unhappy I became at school. For any pretext or other I pleaded illness so that I should not have to go. "Mary is definitely unwell', Dad wrote in one of his letters which I still have. It was through this that a whole new vista of life that was to shape my character and future opened up.

CHANTERSLEUR FARM

All the names of the places where Hugh and Mollie have lived conjure up a feeling of pleasure. They roll off the tongue, 'Ravens Wood', 'Chantersleur' and later, 'Hill Farm'. They all have the taste of the countryside. My school left behind for a term, I was to have lessons with Mollie's children. Kay was then a boy of five, Janet, his sister, only three. Auntie Mollie, as we called her, was a friend of my Father's. She was a trained teacher who taught us at home. Looking back I find it difficult to remember our doings as of any one visit. We were to go there many times. Always the white farmhouse held the same warmth for me. Having been two cottages it was now made into one house. The beamed rooms were joined by a narrow kitchen downstairs, and a small archway up. The dairy was entered by a cool dark passage from the back door. The front door opened straight into the sitting room. Here we would lie full length on the rug after dinner to 'read quietly'. The lights were paraffin ones which cast their soft light on the brown polished wood of the furniture. Bath time was in a tin bath in front of the fire. The logs crackled and flamed as the hot water was added from the kettle hanging above. Auntie Mollie had a way with all the children who were lucky enough to come under her care. Her Australian accent became synonymous to me of kindness. We were happy in our old clothes. The music we heard were the songs and marches that Mollie whistled as she dusted in the rooms above. The milk was brought from the farm buildings two fields away. Separated by the bell separator it would ring it's way through with each turn of the handle. Thick yellow cream came out of one side and skimmed milk out of the other. The skimmed milk was then fed to the pigs. The cream was made into into cream cheese, which was wrapped and weighed and sold to a shop in Reigate. We would ride to town with Hugh and Mollie on the weekly shopping day. Side by side on the back seat of an open tourer we would bounce over the country lanes of the Surrey countryside.

After the term at Chantersleur was over I returned to South Hill

Janet on Quassy with Alice and puppies at Chantersleur, 1936

to another step in my life. Dad realised that for Twins to be considered only in the context of 'as good as' or, worse 'not as good as each other' was a bad thing. Alice and I were to go to Secondary Schools in Birmingham, Alice to Edgebaston College and I was destined for the High School. Margaret my cousin was already there. We were to look different and be different.

We had yet another 'Aunt' in charge of us. She was of no relation, and had been a matron in a boys' prep school. Auntie Olive never became the mother that Beryl had been to us. I always felt she preferred boys to girls. Her first job was to organise our new brown and green school uniforms. It was a slow process fitting us into jerseys, stockings and skirts.

We caught the two buses to Edgebaston each morning at the top of Oak Tree Lane. Due to my tearful reluctance to go to school at all, Alice rode the full distance with me, only to have to return at the terminus to ride back to her own stop. This she did for a number of weeks quite uncomplainingly.

I soon found how very backward I was compared to the other girls at the school. One morning I remember Margaret being brought down from a higher class to see if she could stop me crying. I sensed that knowing that my adopted father was in his eighties, the staff expected he might have died. This made me cry more. I simply felt rather naughty and unforgiven at the fuss I had made that morning.

On the journey home, speed was of the greatest importance. Dad had always warned us that at his age he would not live forever. Some day he would be dead and we must be prepared for this. My headlong dash into the house at tea time would be followed by nonchalance when I had seen that all was well at home.

Dad often took us to visit his friends in Birmingham. Uncle Harrison Barrow and Aunt Ethel, as we called them, were Quakers living not far from us, who had no children of their own. We also went to stay at their cottage on the coast at Harlech. Perched above the sea, it looked down on to the rocky coastline. Nearby was one of the most unforgettable places — a tiny Church almost buried by sand. No houses were in sight round it. For what purpose was it built so far from human habitation? Had the village once been there and had it too been buried by sand?

Uncle Harrison had the most lined face of anyone I had ever known. On asking the reason I was told that it was because of the time he had spent in prison during the 1914 war as a Conscientious Objector. Aunt Ethel was a jolly person. We took it in turns to have Sunday lunch with her. Before a blazing fire I watched her eat a whole box of chocolates in an afternoon! It seemed a delightful debauchery after our one boiled sweet after dinner at home. I, longingly, refused all but one.

Time was however, running out for us and our life with Dad at South Hill did not last very much longer.

TO TALK OF MANY THINGS,
OF SHOES AND SHIPS AND SEALING WAX . . .

My Father loved to quote Lewis Carrol. He would repeat lines of it to us. I can recall useless words about the Walrus and the Carpenter 'walking hand in hand' and 'Seven~maids with seven mops', diligently sweeping for half a year, supposing they could sweep away the quantities of sand. At Chantersleur, Mollie's choice of books were more down to earth, mainly about things which could be done. We became acquainted with Arthur Ransome. In the half light that only a winter's day can bring, we once sat around the huge open fire, before dinner and after dinner, Mollie's gentle voice reading on. We were far away with Kitty, John and Susan on the shores of Lake Windermere. Later I read the R. .M. Lockleys books of this time. I was fired with an enthusiasm to experience the remoteness of the Islands of Britain that he wrote about. Later I was able to visit the Island of Skokholm off the west coast of Wales. It was then owned by the West Wales Ornithological Society. Sailing from Haverfordwest over the notoriously rough stretch of sea I set foot on the windswept wharf to stay on the then no longer permanently inhabited island. Razorbill and Guillemot perched precariously on the cliff edge high above the surf breaking on the rocky shore below. Puffin had taken over the rabbit burrows for nesting, fighting for possession with the petrels and shearwaters. No one who has not held the tiny Storm Petrel in their hands and released it, to wing its skimming way out to sea, can really be said to have experienced true wildness. Much has also been said about the Manx Shearwater and its remarkable homing powers, returning from thousands of miles away to its nesting burrow year after year. It is only as an unscientific observer that I relate my experience of them alighting on a dark night, to drop down in their hundreds amidst the shuffling feathered bodies as they make their way to the sitting birds on the nest. In the bird books their call is described as 'Kuk-kuk-kuk' but the sepulchral croon- ing evokes the same feelings in man as of the thrice time bark of a fox on a still dark night, increased a hundredfold. With the aid of a torch the birds were taken from their burrows to have a British Ornithological Society ring put on their slender legs. With Islands still in mind, later I was to apply for a job on Fair Isle. Recently I heard that George Waterson, the owner, had sold the Island to the National Trust. I was reminded of my audacity. thirty-five years ago. The surprise Mr. Waterson must have felt when his would- be teenage Warden stepped from the train onto the platform at Edinburgh was not shown on his face. Something of the weekend he gave me in recompense for a wasted journey remains in my memory. The Castle, the lush summer trees of the woods and the shores of the Firth of Forth. Sand after sand and the sea where the cries of the Oyster-catcher seemed to hold the past and the future of all things which make one laugh or cry in its plaintive call.

A feeling for the countryside at South Hill in the garden and the field, and later at Chantersleur and Hill Farm seems to have given me a heritage all my own.

I was ten years old when Alice and I were again at Chantersleur Dad, in his eighty fifth year, had become ill in the cold winter months. With the strangeness of memory I do not remember being sent away or of saying 'Goodbye'. Seated round the dinner table we were reading our letters from home. My

Father had died the day before. Resolving that I would not cry I stoically reached the last sentence. Kay, with his thatch of fair hair and rosy face, sitting opposite me, asked cheerfully "How is the old man?" The tears flooded down my cheeks as Mollie hurried us from the table to the quiet of the sitting room. How could my beloved Dad be called an 'Old man?'

Later in the afternoon, as I slowly turned the pedals of the tricycle, I felt years older. I knew that never again would anyone care in quite the same way what I did. From now on I would be responsible for my own destiny.

CHAPTER 2

ANOTHER FAMILY

ANOTHER FAMILY

Alice and I arrived home a few days later to an atmosphere of change. Our few things were to be packed and many discarded, before we caught the train from Birmingham's Snow Hill station to London and then on to Welwyn North. I cannot remember being sad at leaving or even turning to take one last look at the house where we lived for the first ten years of my life. Perhaps it was indeed only a building, now the main character, our Dad, had gone. Alice and I had stayed for several short holidays with Dad in a rented house at Tewin. Now we were to live with our Aunt and Uncle, of no relation, but who were to be our guardians until we were grown up. They had recently moved to a very new architecturally planned house, one of three, built in the fields on the side of the road just outside the village of Tewin. Two beautiful oak trees edged the garden of the first house where my Uncle and Aunt lived. I can picture them now in their summer leaves. We were later allowed to hammer up a platform for our tree house. Also I can see them in my minds eye in their darkest mood of terror, with the fires of the London bombings flickering red behind them. Yet again one of the most rare and amazing sights I was to see behind the dark branches was the Northern Lights or the aurora borealis flickering in tongues of pink, white and green on a never to be forgotten night during our years at Tewin.

The outside of the houses was quite plain, known by the locals as the "shoe boxes"; in reality the light sand coloured bricks ! the one slope roof in grey tiles and the one pane glass of the windows were a glimpse into the future. The wide beds of blue gentians and the roses were a delight of the present.

Nothing of this however was in my mind as yet, and perhaps have only really come to it now I have grown older.

My first real memory of travelling towards our new life at Tewin begins on the train to Welwyn North. Alice and I had been handed over at Kings Cross station and we sat opposite my Uncle Roland in the third class carriage of the steam train. We had some slight conversation, but I, as always, was the master of silence in such a situation, not knowing what to say. As I was to learn later, my Uncle regularly slept during his journey from his work in London from Kings Cross to Welwyn North, and except for one known occasion, woke just in time to get off the train. But I looked in horror, thinking to myself " 'he' has gone to sleep! now what shall we do". Alice seemed unperturbed, but tears filled my eyes and I felt that the end of my world had come. Then we thundered over the viaduct, glimpsing the river Lee below and were pulling up at Welwyn North station to be met, taken home to Sewells Orchard, introduced to a very different life from that which we had just left in a Quaker family.

My Dad had known my Aunt Grace as a young girl and she had lived in his house in Birmingham for some months, as he once said "becoming like a daughter to me". To this family he had turned to take on Alice and myself in the capacity of parents and guardians. He always said he must live as long as possible! and did so until eighty six. It would not be a task one could envy of anyone, to take into a family of three children, all older, and nearly grown up, two more, with a very different upbringing and characters aged only ten, be it only for the school holidays. It had been arranged that we should go to boarding school. I remember being asked "what sort of school would you like to go to?" Standing in the kitchen my answer, running through my own mind, knowing then that only boarding school would be acceptable, was "just an ordinary day school like every other little girl living with their own parents". I did not say the thought out loud however, and soon our green jerseys and skirts were bought and we were packed ready to go to St Christophers School at Letchworth. A modern co-educational School where one could do almost what one wanted except choose which lessons to go to. It was vegetarian, and quite strange meals were produced. For tea we always had baked slices of bread, cut into rusks, an excellent way of using up stale bread no doubt! but said to be for the benefit of our teeth! I have never disliked them however, and I remember coming in just before tea time and grabbing a handful to put me on, when no one was looking. Now when I bake a few crusts for the dogs I do the same and it reminds me of those far off days. I was far from happy there. Alice made friends and liked the school. She had little to do with me and greatly resented me hanging around her trying to share her friends.

I think I was saved from staying there for the rest of my school life by a school report which stated for the subject of Art "As good as her sister". Perhaps this statement was better than "as bad as" — but it would not have been acceptable to my Dad and it was not to my Aunt and Uncle. We were always encouraged to be individual people, not one of a pair. So it was that I joined my Aunt and Uncle's youngest child Nan, at the Quaker School in York "The Mount". Nan was in the top class and had half a term to go before leaving. I being accepted under the usual age of twelve, was only eleven and a half years old, being the youngest and also for a half term the shortest, and probably the shyest! had at least something different from the other girls.

I did however settle in and soon had a nick name, "Littleman". Great hilarity has always followed the name of "Littleboy" the name of my Quaker family. I've often said in later years, that I only married to change my name to a real unlaughable, interesting, English name, with numerous variations, "Hartshorne". I have always loved my kindly name of "Littleman" however. To have a nick name is always a compliment you have been noticed.

Nan talked to me when we met in the corridor. I grew a little taller. We arrived home for the holidays and my Aunt instructed Nan to fit us out with "bras" the size was right and I stayed with it for many years.

In those years just before the 1939 War no-one could believe that another war would be fought. In spite of the Nazi ideas building up in Germany it seemed incredible that any human being could or would be capable of the cruelties and madness that has happened to the World again and again since.

The gently sloping fields and clumps of woodland around us were bright with summer. Bill, the second son of the family, who was of college age, took us swimming. The new baths at

Letchworth were only three quarters of an hour away. It was a pleasant traffic free drive along empty roads in those days. Sometimes we went to the baths at Welwyn, bitterly cold, being fed directly by water from the River Lee. Occasionally we went to the little town of Ware, the very small bath here it was usually deserted and full of leaves.

Leonard, the oldest of the family, occasionally came home on holiday from his job in the BBC, he was Washington Foreign Correspondent for the BBC. The holidays passed quickly and we were all too soon packing our trunks for school.

The family at Tewin were always encouraging to us, but it was our Aunt who always seemed more concerned in making something of us. One of her favourite remarks was "We don't do that" which I thought probably meant that WE might. Probably my worst fault was "answering back" or fighting my sister Alice. Al and I were constantly scrapping. I have learned of course, since, with my own children and grandchildren that fighting rarely means anything to the children, but can be extremely annoying to grown ups! Once sitting by the fire in the long light sitting room with its windows looking out over the lawn and distant fields and woods she told me "I think I may be able to make something of you, but I am not sure about Alice". I do not know what prompted this statement as Alice generally seemed more favourable material to work on than myself.

We loved to be off on our bikes, the river Mimram was a favourite place for watching Snipe and Redshank who flew up in great numbers with their tumultuous cries. I became keen on bird watching and although not expert I could already identify most birds by sight or sound. The attraction was freedom, gumboots and old clothes. My Aunt was also very good at recognising birds. This we did have in common. One summer morning we both got up at five to hear the dawn chorus. The mist was just receding as the summer sun was rising over the fields. The pheasant called her beautiful evocative call. When I hear it now I am reminded of that morning.

My Uncle encouraged me to buy a pair of Ross binoculars and

Above: *The sheep at Hardwick House Farm in the winter of 1995.*

Below: *The hens.*

Above: *The trees in winter.*

Below: *Tommy Pearson.*

Above left: *Winnie the teddy bear was put in Rigmor's suitcase by Alice, aged 8, when Ringmor left South Hill, where she had been looking after Alice and Mary in 1933.*

Above right: *Alice with James, her first grandchild, June 1976.*

Left: *The hawthorn tree 1980. Mark, Richard and Seth with Tessa.*

Above: *Mary with Robert driving the newly restored red President tractor at Hardwick House Farm 1966. (Photo by Jean, Robert's wife.)*

Below: *A snow storm blowing up at Burnsall on the way to 'the fourteen gate road'. February 1990.*

the five volume *Hand Book of British Birds* by Witherby Jourdain Ticehurst and Tucker. The first volume was due to come out and I eagerly awaited the last book to be printed, constantly urging Uncle to call at Foyles on his way back from his work, as a director of the Scientific Instrument Makers "Casella's" to see if it was ready. I was extremely lucky to have the money, be it in my Uncle's care. The twenty pounds for the books and the twenty for the binoculars would have been a fortune to some people then! but has given me immeasurable pleasure since. The books are still one of the very best books on ornithology that has been written. One afternoon I remember being allowed to boil up a pigeon and a frog in an old pan. I had found them dead in the fields. The idea was to get all the bones clean and wire them together in their upright forms. The smell was disgusting. Later Uncle arrived home from work with a bottle of Hydrogen Peroxide, saying that I would have to bleach the bones white or the job would not be done right.

Even I was horrified at the abandon with which he tipped the whole lot into the wash hand-basin saying that it would be quite alright! I was quite used to being told to go back and wash the basin after washing my hands and leaving a black rim around it. Could it really be alright?

Eventually the skeletons were done and stood well on their boards. With these and maps of the Starling roosting trees, which I had drawn up from dusk cycle rides around the area, I returned to school to win a prize.

It was the first time that Starlings had been accused of spreading foot and mouth disease to farm animals. The British Ornithological Society had asked for members to plot maps and send them in, to see if anything could be learned from the numbers of birds in an area corresponding to the numbers of farms affected.

In the summer holiday of 1939 Rigmor, who had looked after us so well at South Hill wrote and asked if Alice and I could go to Denmark to stay for a few weeks at the school where she worked. It was an exciting trip from Harwich to Esbjerg and then across to

Jutland and Copenhagen to stay in the old castle at Jaegerpris, a school for girls.

We all had bikes and we set off for rides along sandy sunny paths through woods. Everyone was friendly to us and we learned the pleasures of eating fruit soup and open sandwiches. We had hoped to visit Copenhagen, but Rigmor received a telegram from Uncle which said "send the twins home". We arrived home and a day or two later war was declared. Many things were to happen to Rigmor before we heard from her again after the war was over. Denmark was occupied by the Germans. Her mother hid a Jewish girl in the attic of their house until the country was free. I have kept in touch with Rigmor for over sixty years and a great friendship grew up between us. South Hill and its occupants had been a shared experience. I never visited or met her in person again, but my daughter Tessa and her husband went camping in Denmark in 1988. They called on her at her flat and had much to talk about over an "English" cup of tea. How interesting she was and how she would have enjoyed to read this story. Rigmor had a lot of success with the stories she wrote. One of the last letters she sent me enclosed a worn photograph of the teddy bear which Alice and I had stuffed into her case before she left South Hill "to keep her company on the journey". As she said in the letter "he had heard many stories".

HILL FARM

Alice and I went many times to stay with Hugh and Mollie during our childhood in Birmingham, and after we had left. We always received the same welcome, as though we were really wanted there. I was into my teens before I realised that, being paid for, we were a source of revenue, not just invited relations! The realisation came as a slight shock to me. but by that time our friendship was firmly established.

Of all the animals on the farm, excepting Betsy the brown and white spaniel who could almost be called a celebrity, so well did

*Jaegerpris, Jutland, Denmark 1939. Setting out on a bike ride.
Alice (left), Mary (right), and Ringmor*

she under-stand what was said to her; I remember best the two ponies Quassey and Quanser. They were Mother and son; by no stretch of the imagination could they be called well broken in. Straight from Exmoor their mealy brown noses were always sniffing the wind for something to excite them. Janet could catch and ride them round the field at the back of the house.

Quanser was sold, but Quassey lived for several more years in the field behind the house at Chantersleur.

Eventually when the family moved to Somerset, Quassey went with them. In the orchard under the cider apple trees Janet rode him until she was too heavy for his slender back. Idleness made him more mischievous and he went to live at the farm where Hugh worked as Estate Manager. The farmer's son, David, would be able to leap if unsuspected, onto Quassey's back for a wild bare back ride. Every now and again the soft Exmoor air would blow from the moors not far away and Quassey would throw up his head and push through the nearest hedge to freedom. The cry would go up, "Quassey is out again."

The house was within travelling distance of Hugh's job. Built of grey stone, with a slate roof, it nestled among the hills a few miles from the Devon border. The stream which flowed directly below the fields and orchards was the home of Dipper and Kingfisher. As one stood beside it, the chatter of water over pebbles would block all other sounds from the ears. The white fronted Dipper would flit from stone to stone to dive and reappear here and there as its erratic course was followed from the bank. Always the huge wedge winged Buzzard, so much a bird of the West Country, would wheel and cry, her plaintive mewing call echoing across the woods and hills. An occasional sortie down for a vole or mouse, accompanied by a dark brown flapping bird, who rose again out of the grass, to show just what a magnificent size she was; and how high she flew, appearing as she generally did, as a tiny dot in the sky.

The barns behind the house lay in a cobwebbed silence of spent oat husks and unused whisps of hay. Once in a while farmer Gamlin would bring his accordion and the empty barn would

come alive to the sound of old fashioned dancing. The jolly cor-
duroyed figures and farmer Gamlin's wife, standing in her long,
dark skirt, head scarf framing her beautiful face almost seems to
be a picture out of history.

One has only to see the same brown polished furniture, which
has reflected the firelight for over fifty years; the green set of
drawers where the gloves were kept; to smell the mingled wood
smoke of the sitting room fire, the soap of the bathroom, to be
transported back in time.

Of the many visits I made, with Alice and later, alone, as the
train's whistle blew for departure at Paddington to head towards
Reading and on to Bristol, the very air seemed to change to lazy
Somerset softness, breathed in from no other place in the British
Isles.

As children we cycled along the high banked lanes, or rode the
pony Quassey. One night we asked to sleep out in the hay loft
above the cider press, from which, as the tickling hay exasperated
me, I escaped in the very early morning. Across the cobbled yard
and up the creaking steps to the apple room, where I was sleeping, not even the feel of the cool, soft sheets could keep me from
getting up just once more, to lean my elbows on the sill of the
tiny window, to breathe in the wild fast dash of the chattering
Swallows, darting in and out of the eaves. In the morning I was
considered very unsporting not to have finished the night out. To
me the sight and sound of the Swallows easily out weighed the
other children's criticism. I still think of that magic morning
when I first heard the dawn chorus of swallows. Another summer morning I remember Janet's tears of dismay when a red coat-
ed bullock took the gate on its horns, to lie in a tangled heap in
the yard. Hastily summoned, the sound of farmer Gamlin's hob
nailed boots rang out on the stones of the drive. He tramped
round the corner of the house, red faced and cheery, as he told us
all would be well. There must have been many drawbacks to living far from the shops or neighbours for Mollie. The drive to
work must have been treacherous and dark on a winter morning
for Hugh. Often the water, pumped from below the house by a

petrol engine, would run out. Frequently it was Monday and wash day. All would have to wait just as it was in the sink, until his home coming. But for us, all too quickly the holidays would come to an end and we would be on our way back to school, with only just enough time to hastily throw our things into a trunk.

1939 – 1945

Autumn had come again and Alice returned to school at Letchworth, where I caught the train from Welwyn North up to York. It was thought that bombings would quickly start, in fact two years went by before people not of an age to be called up or go into industry were greatly affected. Also everyone had the idea that it would be a quick war which turned out not to be the case.

Nan left university and went to work in a munitions factory near Boston Spa. What a strange place to have a munitions factory. It was, however, unexpected and hidden in woodland and fields. After the war it became a giant trading centre and by its very isolation could be seen as a good place to choose. It was a depressing place. Although my Aunt said it was dangerous work, Nan made light of this. It was hard for many young people of the call-up age to interrupt their training, apprenticeships or jobs. A lot was made of fighting for one's country and very little of the terrible carnage which was to follow. Alice and I were lucky to be still at school which went on as usual.

It was suggested that we might be evacuated to an American Quaker family. Alice firmly put her foot down on this however; her headmaster had said that to go would be very wrong and cowardly. This was accepted by the family and very glad I was that I had someone to say No for me. I was able to continue my schooling at The Mount and holidays with the Miall family in Hertfordshire.

Bill was a conscientious objector and joined the Friends Ambulance Unit. Leonard was working in the BBC and through

Roland Miall in the sitting room, Sevells Orchard, 1940, taken by Mary.
The Brownie camera was on books on the table and Uncle gave instructions as to when to open and close the shutter

his work and other overseas newsworkers, people all over the world could tune in, often from hidden lofts, attics or castles, to the pips of the BBC news broadcast. The few bars from the Beethoven Fifth Symphony, which transcended all languages, became the rallying call of a whole generation of lover-s of freedom. The relief of hearing these voices from an occupied country is inestimable. Uncle did not have any religion, telling us he was an Agnostic. Like my Dad he was one of the very fine people, with firm and true ideals.

Ration books were issued and we had to carry our identity cards and gas masks. As we lived in the country extra milk, cream and butter could be easily obtained if the money was there to buy it. At school we had our first taste of margarine which was not very nice, spread on slices of bread for tea with nothing else might seem a poor meal today, but to us it seemed reasonable.

During these years we visited Malham, staying at the Youth Hostel, walking the five miles from the station at Gargrave. The country with its wild beauty was deserted. hills were a pleasure to walk in, as they are still today.

At home food was harder to get and I was once asked to go and get some fish from a shop in the little town of Ware. The journey was several miles on my bike, from the start I felt it might not be a very successful shopping trip! but never the less I set off. I had not gone far when I met two boys whose mother was a great friend of my Aunt. Both boys were very keen bird watchers, one was a little older than I and one younger, and although I had hardly ever spoken to them in the presence of the grown ups, we all stopped and they said that they were going to Bramfield woods to birdwatch. "Come with us' they said, pictures of nuthatch. tree creepers, nightingales passed before my eyes, but I said "No, I've got to go and buy fish" and as an after thought "I'll meet you here at the end of the path on the way back". I reached the small deserted main street of shops. All the doors were closed, blinds drawn, no-one was walking about to ask where fish could be bought. It looked more like Sunday than fish day. I walked, pushing my bike the length of the street and back again, without seeing a single person or fish. I decided that it was a wasted journey and that I had better get back to Bramfield as quickly as possible. I cannot remember seeing any bird of special interest, but it was a rare thing for me to be out with any one of my own age. We were very lonely children when we were at home from boarding school, as we had no friends. This alone was enough for me to decide, even if I could afford it, that boarding school would not be for my children.

It was near!y dinner time and I reached home. My Aunt was frantically worrying about what we would eat, when I told her there was no fish and described the empty street, followed by the delights of company at Bramfield Woods her answer was "I don't believe you Mary, you have not been to Ware". How hard it is not to be believed when you are telling the truth. I hastily assured her that we would be perfectly happy to eat bread and cheese, we didn't care for fish, It still felt good to have been asked out to bird watch with experts. When we were asked "what would you like for pudding" during those years we always said "cornflakes and cream", this was easier, everyone was happy. cream had only to be fetched from the farm a few hundred yards up the hill.

The months were passing and Alice and I were both in the School Certificate years. We at the Mount had been evacuated to Cloughton near Scarborough for two terms by the seaside. We returned to York because there seemed more danger of bombing at Scarborough. Shelters had been made situated between the school and the railway line. We had very many nights when the siren went. We would all troop down in dressing gowns to await the all clear. Very few bombs actually hit York, except one night the station was bombed, the night before we were due to return to school.

My abiding memory of the time was the double summer time and of the very light evenings. Lying in bed learning my School Certificate notes for the exam I watched the evening sky turn faintly to pink. Above the grey slates of the roofs of the tall grey buildings wheeled the swifts, shrieking and turning with acrobatic gracefulness and speed. The summer seemed a never ending one with the beauty of the swifts and the horror of what we heard of the war. When the sunset had gone, the wail of the siren would chill the heart. The sound still gives me the same eerie feeling when I hear it today.

One teacher at The Mount was Miss Ruegg – 'the Egg'— an unforgettable character. Small and intense, she was both loved and feared. Said by the girls to have lost her lover in the 1914–18 war, she appealed to us as a romantic personality. Many of the women of her years did remain spinsters, after the war had taken so many young men. The 'Egg' did much to foster my love of reading and my attempts at writing, the disgrace of low marks in other subjects being partly relieved in English through her encouragement. Her most endearing habit took place about twice a term, and had gone on in her classes throughout the years. Some of her regular stories had, I guess, been heard by the mothers of girls who were now in school! Entering with some book or other tucked under her arm, marked at the appropriate places, she would exclaim 'Today I am going to read you a story. Put your heads down on your arms, close your eyes and listen!" Whilst perhaps many of the girls idled away their hour in the darkness of their folded arms, I would miss not one word of her beautiful Scottish pronunciation. Although at this time I can remember none of the actual tales, or titles, they all had some gripping poignancy, or vital truth, that would move the heart to deep feeling or reflection for days afterwards.

Perhaps my finest hour was a lesson in which my essay on 'An Unforgettable Scene' was read to the class, as an example of what she had wanted from us. It was a description of the brightly polished silver knives and forks laid out on the snowy white linen table cloth in our dining room at South Hill, Birmingham, in the way I like best to remember it.

Eventually Alice and I passed our subjects in the exam, surprising both ourselves and others. Summer holidays were here again.

The nights were full of the drone of the Lancaster and Wellington planes going out to spread their fearful devastation in Germany. Indiscriminate destruction was caused, killing many thousands of defenceless people in small homes, both in London and abroad. As dawn broke the planes returned lighter in weight, quieter in sound and often fewer in number. Bill was reported missing and anxious weeks were ahead waiting to hear news of him. Each morning my Aunt waited for the postman to bring a letter of hope. I hung about the doorway in the sunshine hoping for the best, but my gauche teenage words were of little comfort. At last we did hear that he was alive, and my Aunt and Uncle were able to write and hope again. Alice and I also put pen to paper and did our bit. A code, which I believe originated in a letter from Bill, was used. The name of a German girl, Renarta, was the key word. If the Germans were doing well, Renarta was well. Eventually we were able to say that Renarta was ill. At last Britain was winning, the war would soon be over. Alice and I tried this code too, and eventually our letters would be sent off to Stalag whatever . . . , to this day the rashness of letting us write without seeing what had been written was astounding, for if anyone could get a person shot by letter, it would be me. Perhaps the letters were never received. I do not know. It was many months, and a spell in a German prison camp later, before Bill did return to England. I imagine that the fact that the Friends Ambulance Unit, unlike the normal POW, were allowed to work amongst the wounded whilst in prison had a lot to do with Bill being able to return relatively unscathed at least outwardly. The experience of nursing set Bill off towards becoming a first-class doctor and specialist in his subject.

Term for Alice and myself started yet again. We set off in our different directions still keeping in touch by letter and thought. I had decided that I would study Agriculture thinking that this would allow me to have an interesting outside style of life. I wanted to do something useful, everyone was working to help the war effort. I left school to do a practical year of farming before going to Reading University. When Hugh took on his new job of Estate Manager of several farms in Somerset, west of Wellington, Alice and I had our first visit to Hill Farm. I spent a year working on the farm. I used to cycle to work along the lanes to reach the farm which was set beside a long water meadow, the hills rising around the cluster of buildings. In winter we took a hurricane lantern from behind the door to shine a dim light over the sleeping, chewing red cattle. My first lesson in milking took place under a red cow at the end of the standings. It would have made a Veterinary Officer of clean milk production wince! A liberal amount of spit on the hands to make them slip easily over the teats, followed by the head resting gently against the smooth warmth of the cow s flanks. Here I was to sit, on my three-legged stool, until the udder had the feel of kneaded dough ready and worked for the oven. Nowhere else have I heard this description of how an udder should feel, but nowhere could a likeness be found more applicable to the soft giving warmth a cow should have when milked out. Now and again the farmer, his brown eyes twinkling, would return along the length of the byre, to see how I was getting on. Peggy, the land girl, had everything organised for her milking. She would tackle the most difficult cow without turning a hair. A brilliant scholar in civilian life, she had taken to farming with an efficiency that was hard to imagine possible. After milking was over we would drive the trailer and tractor up the steep hillside to throw out mangels to the bleating sheep and lambs. Or we hoed thistles from the wheat fields. No job, however difficult, could stem Peg's flow of conversation. We rebuilt the world many times, up on the sloping fields in the bright sunshine, or in the damp drifting across from Exmoor. I treasured the thick land army coat she gave me and the memories it evoked for many years after I left Somerset.

The boss had two sons; the eldest had just left school. He was already in charge of the machinery. He must have been eminently suited to more modem farming. His younger brother, like his father, with the same twinkling brown eyes, was a boy for animals and showed his skill with them on many occasions.

Out with the tractors, I would follow with the harrows, doing what I was instructed. Often, the younger boy's serious approach to work was difficult to put up with from someone younger than myself. It was not without reason that I remember the boss coming to me one morning with the request that 'I was not to tease Kenneth again when we worked together . With difficulty I persuaded him to give me a trial drive on the more powerful tractor he drove while ploughing. Nothing can match the experience of a clean silver share cutting through the soil behind you, to return it, in a continuous line against the previous row at exactly the right angle. Behind, the gulls and finches gathered from miles around to feed in the newly turned earth. Farming has changed so much today that it hardly remains a way of life that it seemed to be in the early 1945's. The days of cutting the corn with a binder, and letting the stooks stand to hear the Church bells ring three times before it is led in are over. So are the hay times, when the slow process of traversing the field with frequent breakdowns was only relieved by the passing of the stone cider jar around the band of workers. Life was hard for the boss. As the clouds blew up from the west, with the forewarnings of rain from the Atlantic, the spoilt hay was turned many times by hand on the small steep meadows. Nothing but good has come to the farmer with the invention of modern machinery. Modern drugs and vaccines for the livestock have saved hundreds of animals which previously would have become yet 'another little patch of docks and nettles to remind him of his failures'. The men themselves have not changed all that much. More scientific, better informed, but still they have the same dedication to their stock and land which I saw when I first started farming in Somerset.

Dinner time would see us all in the small stone flagged kitchen, sitting round the scrubbed table in front of the warm range. Sharp-tongued, the boss s wife would scold and chivvy her family to their places. Her brusque voice would tell us 'it is only Queen's pudding today — easy to make as it's wash day . I still smile and marvel to myself that Queen's pudding could be considered 'easy' with the topping whipped to perfection by hand. As the chatter silenced and the kettle gently hissed out its steam over the peace of the dinner hour, she sat at the end of the table, hand in hand with the boss. It was an affection that her sharp tongue almost belied. Looking back, it was strangely prophetic of the short time she had to hold him to her. He was to die a very few months after I left the farm in Somerset to commence my course at Reading University.

I soon found that my choice of course, Agriculture, was unwise. Most girls chose dairying. I was one of three amongst a lecture auditorium of men; most hoping to delay or avoid call-up by working on their fathers' farms. I remember no tutorials of any kind. We took copious notes and answered questions flung at us from our lecturer, who took great delight in putting the three girls 'on the spot'. At the end of the first year I felt I had done reasonably in the exam but soon learned that it was not well enough to stay on the course. It was goodbye to Reading and I left my two companions to their destiny, both to inherit big estates.

I got a job on a dairy farm in Hertfordshire near to my home. Milking was still done by hand. A vivid memory is one of sitting under a cow when the sound of the motor of a flying bomb came directly over us and stopped. The silence was the warning that the bomb was about to drop. Luckily it missed us and came down with a clump nearby.

One of the most beautiful sounds which I heard from the garden at Sewells Orchard at this time was the nightingales singing. On a warm night in June they would start up at dusk, setting off others from various comers of the garden. Leaning out of the window, the scent of my Aunt s flowers and the warm damp grasses enhanced every sound. In the daytime, in the coppice behind the oak trees, the little brown birds would peck about in leaves by my feet; or burst into song from a branch just about level with my head. The woods which came right down to the gardens in Welwyn and Bramfield were alive with their songs. Sadly the building of houses and motorways has largely destroyed their habitat. I think it would be difficult to find one today, however perfect the June night was for song.

After six months near home I moved to a job on a farm near Stranraer in Scotland. Alice, had arranged for me to work with her friend Elizabeth, who was running her father's farm while he recovered from a heart attack. Our first job after I arrived was to help Elizabeth paint the house. High up the ladders we painted the windows, gutters and the drain pipes in green. When we finally reached the ground again we decided that we had done a good job.

It was a lovely dairy and arable farm with the grey buildings clustered around a large white house. We were a jolly crowd, which included a sister, a ginger-haired cousin, a younger brother, ten years of age, called Patrick and several farm workers. I felt rather sorry for the boy. He was always referred to in hushed tones. When I asked why this was so they proclaimed Oh well, he will never be half as good a man as his father is. During my time there he once went off with his mother and father to Glasgow for some reason. His mother returned triumphant because Patrick had not had to be told to take his hands out of his pockets! It seemed such a shame that after three older sisters this attractive lad was such a disappointment to them all. Elizabeth's mother seemed to work late into the night cooking and baking in the kitchen below my bedroom window. I still think of her as 'that poor woman'. When my small amount of cooking or washing seems to be overwhelming I still say to myself 'at least you are not as unlucky as that poor woman .

Life was quite pleasant on the rolling hills surrounded by the sea looking down to Port Patrick or the Isle of Mull. The harvest went well in sunny weather. The sheaves of wheat were cut by a horse and binder. We all stooked them, standing sixteen sheaves together in two rows, leaning together in neat rows up and down the field.

Deciding that I would not go on working for no money, only my keep, for very much longer, I had applied for a job at the Oaklands Farm Institute at St Albans. I was waiting for a reply in case I was lucky enough to be able to leave The Mains as the farm was called, before winter. One evening we were all in the sitting room in our various armchairs or stools waiting to hear a speech from King George VI. I cannot remember now what the occasion was. The speech was given, 'God Save the King' began to play, everyone jumped to their feet in horrifying supplication except for myself. Taken a little unawares by the suddenness of their obedience, I just sat wishing to be swallowed up by the floor, but vowing that I would not act in such a stupid way. Next morning the ginger haired nephew had been straight to his uncle to tell him of my disgraceful behaviour. I was summoned to his office and told in no uncertain terms that if I ever did that again I would be sent straight from his house. I was quite unaware until then of the fierce loyalty that some of the Scottish people held for the English Crown. Soon after this my letter from Oaklands came and I was offered a job, to start at the beginning of the next week. I packed my rucksack again, and took the night train from Stranraer back to Welwyn North to spend a night at home before looking for a room to rent opposite the Institute in St Albans. In retrospect it was probably my last night at my home in Tewin. The war was coming to an end, which it did in the August of 1945. My Aunt and Uncle were soon to retire and move to a cottage in the lovely North Yorkshire village of Lastingham.

CHAPTER 3

MY OWN FAMILY

OAKLANDS

Oaklands was the Hertfordshire County Farm College. Here under the auspice of the War Ag they worked together under the Ministry of Agriculture during the war. The object was to obtain the very best production of food in the British Isles that was possible. It was costly and difficult to import food from abroad. The German U boats were always ready to sink ships on the seas. Many a tractor ordered from America never actually reached these shores; similarly butter from New Zealand or meat from Argentina, our source of these products, was uncertain.

The War Ag ordered village greens to be ploughed up and potatoes to be planted. They even had the power to take a farm from its owner if they thought it was not being farmed sufficiently well.

I was employed on the Poultry Unit where the hens were trap nested to determine which birds laid the best sized and shaped eggs for a breeding programme. We went round every hour to let the hens off the nest and to write their number on the eggs. The work was interesting. The students were the school leavers who came for practical training to our unit. My direct boss was a pleasant girl, Judy, a little older than myself, from Grantham. Eric, the cowman s son, stirred a huge barrel of meal with water twice a day to make a mash. We had many a joke with him as he tried to get the breadcrumb consistency that Judy demanded.

As the war came to an end our students changed to ex-army personnel wishing to take up farming at the Government's expense. Our boss was a Scot, Mr Black, and his pretty secretary, who looked too good for work, was called Sheila. They both usually appeared from an office above an incubator room which opened on to a road which traversed the College grounds. Once a week 500 chicks hatched in the incubators and were sexed by an expert. It was not long before I discovered Sheila at her lethal work. The cock chicks were all flung into a cardboard box on the ground at the back of Sheila's car; a hose was connected to the exhaust pipe and the little fluffy balls were gassed. A shocking waste during a time of meat rationing I thought. One day I decided that as no-one wanted them I would rear 12 in an old hut behind the hen houses. They grew well in their illicit home, until someone approached the hierarchy, who like all people in high places, threatened instant dismissal if the cockerels did not go. Desperate to find a new owner, one of the other workers, a boy working on the land, said he would take them home. I asked for no money but the boy insisted on taking me to the pictures for payment. We spent a pleasant evening watching a film at the picture house in St Albans.

On cold mornings we would stop at the War Ag department for a chat with the pig men. A huge coke boiler heated the vats of food. Near here was the canteen where we went for a cup of tea and a bun at mid-morning. One of the first people I met was Jim, also having a cup of tea. He had just come south to take up a job as tractor driver. Fresh faced with clear hazel eyes he looked the nicest person on the farm. I asked him where he came from. He said Yorkshire and I answered I come from Yorkshire . His look of disbelief told me that he did not think that it could be true. Could anyone with a southern accent as mine come from Yorkshire?

After some months I transferred to the dairy department. The farm was out-lying from the main buildings, over fields that undulated pleasantly. The cycle ride was pleasant and further than it had been to reach the poultry unit. The winter of 1947 however was a bitterly cold one with deep snow for a number of weeks. It was very hard to get up for work at 5.30. in the morning; and with this my second brush with nepotism came.

The Principal's nephew worked on the dairy unit but he was allowed to start at 7.30. in the morning. I plucked up the courage to go to the Principal and ask if I could do the same. The answer of course was 'No, if you do not like it you can leave!'. I liked the farm and the six toed cat who haunted the dairy. I even got on quite well with the cowman, who was Eric's father, and a crusty old codger. He lived in a cottage next to the farm buildings. Eventually he became ill, the students disrupted his routine — they were now airforce men who had been demobbed and thought that they knew more about farming than anyone else.

The scourge of contagious abortion, which in those days was rampant, reached Oak Farm and every calf that year was born dead and was buried in quick lime. The cowman had to leave work with ill-health.

My next boss was Jim, sent down to take charge of Oak Farm. We worked well together but I did do one very dangerous thing for which I received a severe scolding. The farm owned a very unreliable horse. He had been used by every Tom, Dick or Harry, who tried to harness him up to the cart. One day, by climbing on to the manger, I managed to get a collar over his head and the horse into the cart. Jim and I climbed in but instead of sitting down on the floor of the cart I foolishly sat on the side over the wheel. We set off at a spanking pace, the wheel hit the gatepost and I promptly fell over backwards off the cart. Not under the wheel I am able to say — something which ended many lives. Jim did not speak to me again that day.

One morning as we rushed down the undulating hill to Oak Farm on our bicycles Jim shouted back to me and on the wind came the words 'why don't you marry me?' I laughed uproariously but later I began to think 'yes, why don't I marry him?' His honest open face attracted me, and although we came from very different backgrounds, the same ideals that had been those of my Dad and my Uncle and Aunt were those of Jim's Mum and Dad.

Just before we were both to leave St Albans I received a letter from Fred, a boy who had needed a home in the holidays and used to stay on the farm in Somerset. Fred had served in the army in Malaya and had then gone out to Northern Rhodesia as it was then called. He had been learning forestry and he described his job to me saying that if he could get married he might then be able to get a house. I wrote and told him that I was marrying Jim in a few weeks time and suggested why don't you go and ask Alice. So he did just that, and a few months later they married and went to live in Africa.

Just days after this I once again boarded the train to visit my family. Uncle and Aunt had moved north and had settled into their cottage in their beloved Dales. Uncle met me from the train with the car, the dear old Austin CRO 626, that had taken us all safely about the countryside during the war years. We chatted together as we left Pickering. Falling silent I watched the lovely countryside go by. Suddenly the car began to veer about the road alarmingly. This time I did speak out 'Uncle! Uncle! Wake up, you have fallen asleep' I said.

JIM'S FAMILY

Jim's Mother and Father lived in an end of terrace house in Arksey on the northern outskirts of Doncaster. They had taken it over after the soldiers had been living in it during the war. All the woodwork had been stripped out for firewood and burned. Jim's Mother and Father had been able to buy it, decorate and repair it for a few hundred pounds, a lot of money in those days.

Dad was a coal miner but had been seriously injured in the mine under a roof fall. He had to give up a well paid job at the coal-face where he had been in charge of his 'district', as it was called, with fourteen men under him. The men had a walk of two and a half miles from the place where the cage stopped. Everyone had been pleased to work with Tommy, he was a good and safe worker.

Dad's working days were very nearly over when I got to know this kindly man. When his health recovered sufficiently he was given a poorly paid job on the top. The work was picking out the dross on an endless moving belt of coal. Situated outside at the pit top, it collected all the draughts and rain from round about. He was often not in good enough health to walk the two miles to work.

When Jim was 17 he had been offered a farm of 100 acres to rent with a job for his father with training to become chief forester. Dad refused to do it, his main objection being that he would not be able to stand the flies in the summer woods. I suspect that also the complete lack of money to stock the farm, coupled with a

Nellie and Thomas Hartshorne, 1920

sparse education, had something to do with his refusal. Often his family would not have the required penny a day for each of the seven children to go to school. Dad unwillingly went to school in his older sister's shoes when money was not available for boots, but it was often easier to spend the day in the park than attend school. Like most miners Dad was proud and loved his job.

Mother was a talkative quick-silver person. She could cook a batch of bread or make a dinner out of very little, where others would be hard put to begin to think what to do. The cost of my visit to her house must have been quite a drain on her resources, a thing which I did not think of at that time. Today when I get out the cake tin she gave to me, which is still useful, and think of all the other items (spoons and forks, a small table, an old bed settee which we renovated later with wire netting to make it more comfortable) to furnish our first home, I think of her with great affection.

Jim was a fair mixture of the quick silver and the kind. He had started his life in South Yorkshire in the 1920s. He has many interesting stories to tell of his boyhood and early working years in the Doncaster area, where his father worked. Schooldays were over for him in 1936 when he reached the age of 14. He left his school in Hatfield, which was at that time the best secondary modern school in Europe. Children took their scholarship exams, but only the top three would have a chance of further education. Usually only those who could put teacher or bank manager' on the form which stated the occupation of their father would pass. Summer holidays of play in the fields behind the colliery houses, where the sky larks rose into the sky and corn crakes lead their chicks to drink at the brook, were over.

Thomas, his father, had wanted Jim to go to work in the mines so he went with his Dad to be interviewed for the job of running an engine to draw the trucks from the coal face to the shaft bottom. They waited eagerly, second in the queue, but the first boy was given the job so they went home disappointed. A job had to be found elsewhere. Nellie, Jim's mother was relieved, as the miner s life was one of poor pay, injury and silicosis in later years from breathing coal dust. She was from a Staffordshire farming

72

family and was sure farming would be a better job for her slightly built hard-working lad. A job was found a few miles from home on a farm at Brierly Common. Jim was to live in, and receive one shilling a week, with a new suit once a year. The farmer was named Percy, who, with his brother Jack and sister Miss Eccles, in their seventies, farmed one hundred acres. The day started at 5.30. in the morning winter or summer. A loud knocking on the wall got Jim out of a deep feather mattress, into which he had sunk the previous night, only to fall asleep before there was time to appreciate the comfort. Lit by a paraffin lamp, Jim found that the fire of crackling sticks had boiled the kettle and was ready to mash a scalding cup of tea. This had to be drunk while Percy laced his boots, before going out into the yard to start work. By 7.30. the herd of 20 cows would be milked by hand, feeding of calves, horses and pigs was all accomplished. A few minutes for breakfast and then the field work started.

Each job was according to the season. Mangels were carted in during winter to feed the cattle. Muck was carted out to be left to rot in a large heap in the corner of an arable field, later to be spread into the potato rows at planting time. In spring the field of rye was hoed, to be harvested in autumn and sold to a biscuit factory. Two hay crops were taken followed by harvest. Once, as the binder left a smaller and smaller square of uncut corn in a field, a vixen led her seven cubs out of the corn to safety. Hedges were trimmed and laid, ditches were dug. Each year, after the mares had foaled, the foal would be tethered to the back of the cart to follow its mother in the shafts. This helped to break the youngster to work, also enabling the mare to work and suckle the foal during the day. The land was nurtured long before conservation had become an aim of the 1980s and 1990s.

Jim worked for three years with competence. On his seventeenth birthday he decided to ask for a rise in his wages. His shilling a week had been dutifully handed over to his mother on visits home. Percy however had other ideas — as insurance stamps now had to be paid twopence would have to be deducted from the shilling. Good food and a good bed could be given but money on the farm was in short supply after the year s expenses had been paid. Not long after this Jim got talking to the driver of a tractor in the next field who was doing contract work for one of. Percy's neighbours. He offered Jim a job at ten shillings a week Miss Eccles, who had grown fond of Jim, pleaded with him to stay on with the words 'We might get a tractor one day'. Jim wrote out and handed in his notice, packed his case and despite Percy standing at the foot of the stairs barring his way out, he left. The contract job was to last for seven years during which Jim cultivated many thousands of acres, winter and summer.

He worked throughout the war years over fields, many of which were as large as ninety acres, often remote from civilisation, reached only by green lanes between hedgerows which transversed the area. On winter days the fog would cling to face and coat with no modem cabs to keep the driver warm. In summer the sun was hot, the flies were torment. Often the tractors were kept going throughout the night, with only the head-lights to keep one company.

Many exciting or exasperating things happened — from having to pull out the tractor which had stuck in the clay using a heavy chain tied to a tree, to digging up a medieval forest. Great tree trunks had been buried beneath the peat; the first process in the formation of coal below. A most terrible experience was a burning bomber hurtling through the sky to land, with the charred body of its pilot, only an arm's length away from the tractor.

Progression into other jobs and experiences made Jim an interesting person to talk to and be with. He had moved to the job in St Albans at the Farm College a few months before l got my job there.

With a warning from my Uncle that I was an 'outside girl' Jim willingly took up the challenge of marriage.

OUR NEW LIFE TOGETHER

The weekend at my Aunt and Uncle's cottage in Lastingham was a pleasant change from that of work at the Farm College in St

Albans. I saw the alterations that had been done to the house and garden, we had walks down the hill past the church to the farm and up the hill to the forestry land which had recently been planted with young spruce trees. All too soon it was time to get the train back to London and out again to St Albans to start work.

Jim and I had decided to get married in May of 1947 from his mother and father's home in Doncaster. We would then look for a farm job with a cottage in the north, which we both thought we would like better than the south. Our lives had been different but we were sure we could make a good life for ourselves together. Many of our interests were in ordinary outside things.

We started the journey north on Jim's Vellocette motorbike, with our luggage in the sidecar on a beautiful spring evening. The Great North Road, the A1 as it is now, took us through all the towns that are by-passed today. The pleasant fine stone buildings of Stamford, Peterborough or Grantham are all lost to us, unless a special detour is taken. No longer does the tune of the road change to ancient echoes of buildings or cobble stones, or a sharp turn in Stamford slow our speed to a crawl and an exclamation of 'I know now where we are'. Lost also, although I have not actually driven the route in early May on a warm velvet night to see if it is so, must be the glorious serenade of nightingale song from the roadside verges which were even to be heard above the hum of the bike. We passed their northernmost haunts, just south of Peterborough and arrived in Doncaster very early in the morning.

Three weeks passed until our wedding day which was to take place at the Registry Office in Doncaster. My Uncle and Aunt were coming and had arranged an excellent wedding breakfast in a small cafe overlooking Doncaster market place. Mother and Dad and Jim's young brother Alan, then aged 14, were the only other people to be there. Alice was working and so was Jim's sister. Afterwards my Uncle persuaded my Aunt to go back home to Arksey with Mother and Dad for a cup of tea. We've often tried to guess how they got on. Uncle would have got on very well with Dad.

It was a sunny May afternoon when Jim and I collected the motorbike and sidecar and finally set off for our honeymoon in Scarborough before we took up a job with a cottage in Bishopdale, North Yorkshire.

BISHOPDALE

Jim and I started our married life in a small cottage on the hillside of Bishopdale. The nearest towns were Leyburn and Hawes to the north, and Kettlewell to the south. We could reach these by market bus once a week or by motorbike and sidecar. In those first years after the war everything wanted from a shop seemed hard to come by. For weeks we fruitlessly searched for a simple Jubilee clip to fasten the exhaust pipe on to the engine of the bike — for weeks we had to endure the pipe blowing off every few miles after spending hours with twisted wire or other devices that we thought would be failsafe. It seems quite amazing today when Jubilee clips are to be seen on a card in every ironmonger s shop. We installed our few bits of makeshift furniture in the farm cottage and were delighted to find two grey army blankets and a few white cups in a shop in Leyburn's market square. To buy blankets usually demanded coupons and cups were just not obtainable in the years after the war.

The door of the kitchen opened on to the grassy track leading down to the road below. The curlews nesting on the strip of meadow land by the river gave us a never-ending multiple cadence of song the like of which I have never heard since. It was sad to go back many years later and see that some misguided person had bricked up the doorway. No longer could they stand at the vantage point to listen to that unbelievable song.

Jim started work on the farm. The whole valley observed the farm with interest and regaled us with tales of the manager's lifestyle. They had come from the south and as such were 'off comed ones. Our choice of job proved to be an unfortunate one as it turned out they had really wanted a shepherd rather than

someone to milk the Ayrshire herd. The farmer opposite grateful-
ly seized upon us to help with the hay making. A horse and cart
were sent for our few pieces of furniture.

The small river was forded as no track went up to our next cottage which was situated under the shadow of Buckden Pike.
Inside the back door a high wooden settle protected the circle of
warmth around the fireplace; this was certainly needed as a
howling gale would blow through the house even in summer.
The ancient wallpaper on the stairs would flap about in an alarm-
ing manner inviting the passer-by to catch hold and give it a tug.

During the summer of 1947 Alice was doing a nurses training
course in Birmingham. One of her weekends off was spent with
us. Al caught the train north after work in the late afternoon,
arriving eventually at Buckden, in the dark, by bus. As ten and
eleven o'clock came and went, leaving a paraffin lamp in the window, we fell asleep. We awoke with a start after midnight; there
she stood laughing and looking down on us in our 'wire netting
improved bed'. She had walked all the way from Buckden climbing up, over Kidstone Pass and then down again into Bishopdale
undeterred. But how I asked, 'did you know which cottage to
come to?' The answer was that it was the only house with a lamp
in the window, so she knew that it must be ours She had just
walked in and upstairs! Al lay down beside us and we all fell
asleep until morning.

After working through the hay-making season, Jim and I decided that it might be a better idea to try and buy our own farm and
work for ourselves. We looked at all the advertisements that we
saw in the newspapers. Good farms rarely seemed available and
in any case something little more than £1000 could be considered.
Eventually High Woods Farm came on the market and we bought
it. The keys for the farm cottage were handed back to the
farmer's wife who had employed us. Looking at the windswept
wallpaper, by now a great flapping swathe, she turned to me and
said 'I thought you would have bought some paste and stuck it
back on'. Until that moment I had never even thought of the mys-
teries of wallpaper paste. Jim says that I pulled the paper off but I

say that the damage was done by the howling gales tearing through the door from Buckden Pike.

HIGH WOODS FARM

Druids Cave Farm lay directly below Brimham Rocks; a huge outcrop of millstone grit rocks which were flung down higgledy-piggledy in the ice age, overlooking Nidderdale. Directly below these a grass track, passing through some scrub woodland of alder and hawthorn, went down to High Woods Farm. Previously it had been owned by two brothers who, having fallen out with each other, had divided the house in two. The land had also been divided equally; a half acre was hedged by overgrown hawthorns and belonged to the brother who had received less in his allotted fifteen acres of walled fields. It was said that they never spoke to each other again.

Latterly the farm had been bought by an eccentric living near Ripon who had rented it out to tenants. Sometime two barns either end of the house had fallen in on a windy night killing the cattle housed there. All that remained of these were piles of stones. A newer barn with a loft floor had been built and was a useable shed for tying up cows. The house was in livable order and boasted a good modern range with a water tank that was heated by the fire. There was a flat sink with cold water and a rusty old bath in a cubby hole built of stones off the main kitchen. Beside the fire was a pump from which, backwards and forwards, by hand, water could be pumped up to a tank. The water was pure and had been pumped from beneath Brimham Rocks by a hydraulic ram. It was this seemingly faultless water supply that eventually ended the possibility of us making a living at High Woods. We went into the house enthusiastically in spite of dire warnings from Jim's father, as to the safety of the beam holding the roof at the end of the house. The woodworm eaten stump appeared to have little hold on to any stone and was about ready to follow the barn into obscurity. It did however stay up during

High Woods Farm, 1948.
Jim, Mary and my Aunt, GraceMiall

our time there and beyond.

From the front of the house stretched a view of Nidderdale below. Clocks could be set every weekday by blasting from a quarry not far away, when clouds of dust and rocks were spewed out almost to our boundary. It became a necessity to watch the daily display in case rocks landed on the roof. The farm did have thirty good acres running gently down to a stream which made up for its short-coming.

We bought six pedigree Ayrshire cows and started to sell milk, taking it daily to be collected at the entrance of Brimham Rocks. Our transport was still the motorbike and sidecar with which we fetched coal and groceries from Pateley Bridge. Spending £5 a week on food and paraffin for cooking and lighting, we covered our expenses by the sale of the milk. Life was simple in that no huge bills landed through the letter-box, but the milking was hard work which had to be done twice a day mainly by Jim. We made silage and hay and grew wheat. At that time coupons had to be owned and given for any sort of bagged animal food and we had none as we had not been farming before the war when coupons were first issued. Silage making was a very new idea at that time and we were one of the first to try it. Cutting the grass and tipping it all into the ruined roofless building, we covered each load with molasses from a watering can and trod it down firmly. Eventually Jim fastened it down with a tarpaulin and ropes so that it could not be blown away. When we got it out in the winter with a fork, it made very succulent feed.

The threshing drum was brought round in the Autumn to any farm requiring corn to be threshed. The neighbouring farmers helped at each farm with the hard and dusty job in their turn. We grew a small amount of wheat which could be threshed out leaving us with grain and straw. Although it was hard work all went well and our cows had good calves.

One day Alice visited us in her newly acquired car, a small Standard saloon. Driving up to the foot of Brimham Rocks she stopped the car to look around for our farm. On ascertaining the right entrance she tried to set off again only to find that the car

Above: *View from Pipers Crag to Hardwick House Farm — the 'twenty seven less favoured acres." (Photographed by granddaughter Ruth.)*

Above: *Seth and Ruth on Pipers Crag with Max their sheepdog. Tommy the cat had followed them.*

Right: *Tessa and Catherine with the Galloways on the lower fields.*

absolutely refused to start. Al walked to the farm to find that we had gone out, leaving a note in the letter-box. All she could do in the time available to her was to go back by bus and train to Birmingham. Arriving back home we were dismayed to find what an unfortunate visit her day off had been. Jim rescued the car and managed to start it and bring it home. The Standard had this unfortunate fault until it was finally sold some years later. Al had by now met Fred and they were soon to get married and set out for the forestry job in Malawi, Africa. They left the car with us and it was of great benefit in spite of its unreliable temperament.

The old man at Druids Cave Farm died and his few Shorthorn cows were sold, along with the pigs which had been fed on the milk produced. A way of life which had gone on for many years in great simplicity was ended. To us a good neighbour was gone. Jim had been keen on trying to take on his land into ours. A great opportunity was missed by my urging of caution; the thought of having to take out a loan of nearly £2000 to buy the farm seemed too great. New owners arrived and with them came ducks and hens who all went to drink in the stream which brought our water down from the rocks. As we were new owners selling milk, the water had to pass a test for us to continue. It was devastating to find that the water failed the test and our license was stopped. Today polyurethane pipe would easily have been bought and laid, but at that time it had not been invented and so piping seemed impossible and very costly.

In September 1948 our family was to be increased. I wondered if the car would start and if it would climb up the steep grass track to get me to the hospital. In damp weather the wheels would spin and getting out of the farm could be a problem. On a wild autumn morning at five, the Standard started and climbed up without faltering. I was safely taken to hospital and later that day Kenneth was born, we became a real family. The car had a slight mishap on the journey home however. As Jim opened the door at the entrance to the farm track, the wind caught the door whipping it off the hinges.

Soon Ken was settled into the routine at High Woods. I was

taken up with the task of looking after him. Jim's time was mostly with the farm and its failure or success and he remembers many details that I have forgotten. The Ayrshire cows had good calves. The bull calves were sold, the heifers were kept on for rearing. The milk was fed to the calves and we sold eggs from our hens.

One evening we were planting a patch of potatoes when a telegram was delivered by a telegraph boy on a bicycle. He came across the spring evening fields to us with the sad news that Fred had been drowned in a tragic accident on the Mlange Mountain where he and Alice lived and worked. One week later we met Al and her baby daughter Jennifer aged six weeks at Southampton. They were travelling on one of the last great flying boats. It turned and touched down in a cloud of white sea spray, a magnificent and unforgettable sight, tinged as the scene was with the sadness of Al's grief and our relief at having her and the tiny baby safely home.

COULTON MILL

Without a license to sell milk not enough money could be made to keep us secure and we began to hunt around for more land and a better farm. Very few farms of any worth came on the market at that time, so we did the best we could with the good stock that we had, while deciding what we should do next. Eventually we found Coulton Mill and urged on by my Uncle and Aunt who arranged an overdraft, we bought the farm. We soon found that we had taken on a sheer impossibility. I went to the bank to draw our weekly £5 for the groceries and Ken crawled about the kitchen in one or other of the two romper suits he had to make do with.

Facing page: Jim, Mary and Kenneth 1948

The farm was an old water mill with a well-built water race and still workable mill-stones. An attractive water meadow surrounded by trees led up to the red tiled roof of the mill and house. Behind the land rose fairly steeply to fields that were growing clover and wheat. Little did we realise that the water meadow was to spell doom to our young heifers.

We moved in and Jim settled to hard work. I did what I could whilst looking after Ken. He was now nearly two and we were expecting a second baby in the autumn. We still had no bathroom or electricity and were dependent on paraffin lamps. We decided to put a modern bathroom in and a coke burning cooker to heat the water.

Nearby, up the hill which rose steeply from the front door of the farm house, lived a family called Willis. The teenage son was glad to come and help Jim with jobs that demanded two. One day, thinking they would repair the roof of one of the mill buildings, the boy stood on the top of a wall when it suddenly collapsed inwardly in a cloud of rubble and dust. He was lucky to have been only on the edge and not in the middle. Mr Willis quickly arrived to upbraid us for allowing him to be doing something so dangerous. We were lucky that only one more wall collapsed while we were there and that it was only a dividing wall between two bedrooms not in use. The turning of the mill stones on their inter-acting iron cogs had proved just too much for the worm eaten beams above.

Alice visited us there with her baby daughter Jen. She had found it difficult to settle down to life alone again. Eventually she decided to take a teacher training course. She did well, bought a small house in Welwyn Garden City, and taught in a nearby school for many years.

Once again the water for our farm had to be tested for selling milk. Conditions of the buildings and cleanliness of water were falling under new regulations. Once again we failed the vital test and were banned from selling milk. One morning when Jim went to see if the heifers were alright in the water meadow he found that they had broken the fence into the next door neighbour's

The fallen roof at Coulton Mill

land. They soon became ill and although we called the Vet nothing could be done and seven died. They had been eating ragwort growing in the woods into which they had escaped.

Autumn arrived and Jim had to go into York. As I met him at the door on his return, he held out his hand saying 'Here are the tickets for Australia. I have booked for us to go in April. If you do not come I shall go alone'. By the time our second son, Robert, was born in October I had accepted the idea. In November the farm sale was arranged and everything, except three trunks full of our belongings, was sold and our debts paid off. After the sale I stood in the empty kitchen and looked around. The man who had bought our bed had kindly left our mattress upstairs for us to sleep on that night before we left the next morning. The kitchen was completely bare except for the carrycot on the floor with the month old baby asleep in it. I thought to myself 'what have you done to contemplate travelling to an unknown life twelve thousand miles away with two babies under three'. Next morning as November snow was falling, the car just managed to climb up the hill. We stayed with Jim's parents in Doncaster and then went on to Welwyn to stay with Al and Jen until we were due to sail in April.

OFF TO AUSTRALIA ...

In the 1950s people were encouraged to go and settle in Australia. The fare for accepted men with a trade, such as a plumber could obtain their passage for only £10. We however paid our own fares at about £200 each. Jim was booked into a cabin near the hold of the ship with no outside porthole. I was lucky having a two berth cabin with a porthole. We had made the precaution of getting in touch with a Mr Williams, originally from Wales, who had married Mollie's eldest sister, and he had guaranteed us a job on a farm. We first knew Mollie from our Chantersleur and Hill Farm days. She had come to England from Tasmania as a mother s help to the Miall family.

Jim and Kenneth going to Tasmania on the 'Orcades' 1951

We left Al's house in Welwyn on a spring morning with three trunks, a pram and a carry cot. Sensibly we said goodbye at the door, then caught the train to Kings Cross and thence on to Harwich. The huge white hulk of the Orcades, one of the P&O line, was waiting in dock. She appeared to be so big from the quay that I could not imagine her afloat until we actually felt the swell and heard the creaking of the massive intricate structure. We were rapidly put aboard to witness one of the most emotional scenes ever to be encountered. Coloured streamers linked the families aboard with their families on the shore. Many were in tears, shouting a last fond farewell to parting relatives who were struggling to hear a voice which might possibly never be heard again. This indeed was so with people I was to meet later, who had no hope whatever of making a living and to have enough money to spare to come home again. Glibly people talk today of a better life, a better climate and enough money to fly home every five years, but it certainly was not so in 1951. The almost palpable emotion was a thing I have never forgotten and still confirms my view that to attempt to live under the divided loyalties of home and an adopted country can only be undertaken by a person who is very brave or very foolish. The scene I had witnessed made me doubly glad that we had said our goodbyes at Al's door. The ship set sail and from our cabin the leaving was so gentle and smooth that we only knew the white cliffs were receding when several miles of the twelve thousand, which we were to travel in six weeks, had been passed over.

We were on the tourist deck with many other emigrants. One family I remember particularly. They were Dutch and took up a position for the voyage on deck next to us and our pram where Robert slept contentedly. Of their nine children, the youngest about Ken's age, was attached to the ship by a long strong rope. We talked to them as best we could. We often wondered later on how they had fared. The Bay of Biscay loomed — we were travelling at the cheapest and stormiest time of the year. As expected the sea got rougher, the ship tipped steeply and the crockery which was fastened into a safe shelf nevertheless clattered horizontally from one end of the shelf to the other and back! None of us was seasick and we felt ready for anything by the time Gibralter was reached. We sat on the deck while travelling through the Mediterranean. I spent the time knitting or taking Ken to play in the ship's nursery. We leaned over the deck rails watching the fish leap. So high from the sea were we that we had little contact with the actual waves. It was more like a floating hotel. Port Said was reached and we waited with many other ships for our turn to go through the Suez Canal. The sun blazed down and the hot desert wind brought little relief. Little boats came out to the ship with brightly coloured carpets and leather goods for sale. Eventually we set off along the Canal to Aden, which took two days and a night to reach. The same endless hot sandy shore with an occasional small boat or dark glistening swimmer gave an illusion of distant coolness. We reached the southern end of the Suez Canal and travelled through the Red Sea to dock at Aden. Night had come but we were told we could go ashore.

We walked through the streets carrying the children. In each doorway of the little houses, the inhabitants had rolled out their mats and lay asleep. The warm air and the quiet darkness enveloped us in peace. It was a unique feeling which we will never again experience and one which was unexpected amongst those volatile people. The ship set out again to Singapore, five days and nights across the Indian Ocean without sight of land. Here flew the Wandering Albatross of the southern seas. We were lucky to see two following our ship for several hours; white with black markings, this fourteen feet wing-span of beauty is a relation of the storm petrels. The tiny bird which I had held in the palm of my hand to ring on Stokholm Island off the coast of Wales also covers vast distances across the seas and depicts true wildness. Living on the wing, the albatross only lands to breed on the Pacific island of Tristan da Cunha. Disaster struck when in Coleridge's The Rime of the Ancient Mariner the albatross was shot ...   'And I had done a hellish thing'
... the ship was becalmed in heat and drought, with

'water water everywhere nor any drop to drink and the sailors perished. We did not harm them and were sad to see them veering away towards the south pole. The other bird which we saw was the Frigate bird, deep brown, this bird nests on tropical islands and with its ten foot wing-span and forked tail, twice the length of the body, also roams the oceans. It is related to the homely gannet and is said to foretell hurricanes. No such mishap happened to us.

We crossed the Equator with great celebration. One of the crew, dressed as Neptune, God of the Sea, emerged from the swimming pool at the exact latitude. Ken, then aged two and a half years, remembers the party. We were now in the Southern hemisphere under a southern sky, far more densely covered with stars than our familiar night sky of the northern hemisphere.

We journeyed through the Strait of Malacca to reach Singapore. The main street in the centre of the town teemed with bullock carts, ramshackle cars and people. Suddenly there was a shout behind us and Jim realised it was to him that the shout was directed. Mr Willis appeared, our neighbour from Coulton Mill. It turned out that he lived and worked in Singapore and had only been on leave when we knew him. What a small world it was; to meet a neighbour 6000 miles from home and to have been walking down the street at the same time.

The last part of the journey took us on to the coast of Australia, calling at Freemantle and through the notoriously rough Great Australian Bight to Adelaide, a university town and home of the Black Swan. At the exact hour and minute stated on the timetable the Orcades berthed at Melbourne, Australia. We stayed in a Salvation Army hostel overnight and then crossed the Bass Strait to our new life near Launceston in the north of the island of Tasmania.

HOBART

We spent the next day looking around Melbourne which was very much as any other big city. We could have been anywhere

Singapore 1951.
Jim, Robert and Kenneth

else in the world except for the fact that we were now Pommies amongst the Australian accents. There was still a policy of no entrance for Indian or Asian people, so only our English accent distinguished us from those around us.

In the evening we went aboard the 'Taroona', a small steam boat, notorious for its bucking and dipping as it crossed the 140 miles of the Bass Strait to Tasmania. This small island had been discovered by a Dutch sailor Abel Tasman in 1642. The indigenous population of 5000 were rapidly exterminated, the last dying in 1876. In 1803 the British Empire shipped the first of its 4000 convicts to Van Diemen's land as the island was known. The 26,215 square mile island was a wild beautiful place growing wheat and fruit where the Eucalyptus or Blue Gum trees had been cleared. Sheep, cattle and crops flourished in the more remote north; apple orchards surrounded the southern coastline and on the hillside above Hobart.

After a rough night we arrived at the estuary of the River Tamar in the north. Edging carefully up the river between tree lined shores, we disembarked at Launceston to find that we had now only two trunks instead of three. The most serious loss was Jim's tool box. What the Egyptians or the Arabs would make of the contents — a copy of Fream's 'Elements of Agriculture', or more baffling 'The Kitten' who would not wash its face (a childhood book originally from South Hill), with a beautiful picture of a navy blue night and a great moon shining behind a kitten hanging on a washing line to dry, I could not tell. The Land Army coat would probably be more useful. It could be slung over a camel on a freezing desert night. Luckily we did not need books; and we still had Jim's dressing gown, which my Aunt Grace had insisted we buy from a shop in Pickering — a thing quite unheard of in Jim's household.

We were soon travelling south by train to Hobart. It was wild hilly remote countryside. The line was the most twisting that had ever been constructed. At times the guard's van was almost beside us on the bends. We rocked from side to side alarmingly. At last, late in the afternoon, with two tired children, we stepped out at Hobart Station to an absolutely deserted street. After a few minutes we found someone to take us and our luggage to Mr Williams' house.

The small weatherboard grey house stood on a steep hill overlooking Hobart town. I never did walk much further up the hill, although the road carried on up steeper and steeper with similar little houses on either side. Mr Williams was out but we were greeted by the largest, most asthmatic and kindly person that we were to meet in Tasmania, Ruby, his housekeeper. She quickly made us feel at home, showing me the washhouse across the yard. Here was a water lavatory, a huge copper to heat the water with wood, and a bath and sink to do the washing in. Complete mod cons.

Our stay here was only three nights. Mr Williams thought he could find us a job near Launceston from where we had come. Once again our baggage was packed up and with Mr Williams beside us we again were travelling on the twisting and rocking train.

Arriving once more in the north, a friend brought his car to drive us west along a fertile coastal farming area to the job that was available for us.

The farm was white weatherboard amongst huge cleared treeless paddocks, fenced with wooden rails. The few gaunt, grey tree trunks were like sentinels to the wanton way the timber had been squandered. At the house was a mother and daughter running the farm. Father was, I understood, ill and dying in a back room. This apparently was not quite so, Jim tells me he appeared the next morning sitting on a bench tying up his boots. At any rate I never saw him.

The very first thing that happened after entering the kitchen while Mother made us a cup of tea was that I became aware that the tiled floor was awash with half an inch of water. Instantly I suspected Ken, a two and a half year old toddler with clever fingers Should water be on the floor?' I asked. Mother was horrified — all the water came from a huge galvanised tank on the verandah, piped into the kitchen with a small tap at floor level. If we

Rock Fields, Chudleigh Estate 1952

were to stay there that must never happen again Mother told us. The tank had to supply the house for many months of rainless days.

After a meal we were shown a wood cabin, little more than a derelict hen hut surrounded by waist high weeds, with a door swinging on broken hinges. I thought it could never be repaired well enough to house us. It was decided we were to be taken on and slept the night in a bedroom at the back of the house.

Before he left us, Mr Williams left his telephone number with me, saying that he would be there until one o'clock next day. If there were any problems I could get in touch with him.

In the morning Jim went out to work on the farm while I and the children spent the morning under Mother's feet wondering how we could be kept busy for weeks and weeks until a house, which never would be a house, was rebuilt. Dinner time came and we sat at the table. What were we to do? I looked at my watch, it was nearly one o'clock. Suddenly I leaped to my feet, ran to the telephone and dialled the number. I told Mr Williams 'We can't stop here, it's dreadful'.

An hour later Mr Williams arrived in the car. He had found us a much better job with a house not far from Deloraine. He would take us to a shop to buy the few essentials we needed to set up house. As we drove away Mother stood on the lawn in front of the house with a saucepan in her hand. She looked like a wicked witch silently putting a curse on us. In my worst moments I can still see her standing there. I had only just summoned up the courage to telephone Mr Williams in time.

THE CHUDLEIGH ESTATE

The farming estate where Jim was to work was 2000 acres; most of the land having been cleared from the bush, with a few hundred acres remaining of trees and mountain land rising behind the little settlement. The workers' houses and the manager's more substantial house were timber built with verandas, and galvanised roofs; and the all important galvanised water tanks standing beside the house to collect the only water from the roof. The paddocks were often large, 20 acres or more and fenced with wooden rails. The main tree was the gum, standing tall and grey-trunked, with the drooping, dusty leaves longing for rain. As in all of Australia the grey gaunt stumps of the dead gum trees dotted most of the land, a monument to the wastefulness of man who had, with unthinking speed, chopped and felled huge quantities of timber, with little thought of replanting for the future generations. Even in the 1950s when we were in Hobart, ships from Russia came in stacked with timber for building, in exchange for butter or meat. Rolling hills were the main feature of the west coast of Tasmania.

We moved into our house, which had two bedrooms and a kitchen with a fireplace, but no running water, sink or bathroom. My main task every morning was to chop wood from a huge pile of branches which were brought to supply us with fuel. Every morning dawned with a cold white frost, which by ten o'clock would melt away into a cloudless, hot sunny day. Amongst our two chairs, a mat and a bed, cot and pans and cups, we had bought a primus paraffin burner, which as in our days at High Woods was our main means of boiling our kettle. The wood burning stove required quantities of wood to keep it burning for any length of time.

Jim's job was that of tractor driver and he spent many hours ploughing and reseeding the paddocks with horse or tractor. Sheep were the chief enterprise of the farm. The 100 Leicester rams were crossed with the Merino for meat production and wool. A few cows were kept to supply milk to each family. These calved and were then allocated to the paddock beside each house and were the responsibility of the family.

We milked our Jersey cow and made butter and had our own milk supply. Meat was also supplied; a quarter of a sheep every two months and a quarter of a beef animal twice a year. We had no electricity for refrigeration. The sight of so much mutton in a hot climate can become quite nauseating after a very few days.

Looking towards the farm

Ken's reaction as I put his dinner down on the tray of his high chair was to throw his plate upside down on the floor; My reaction, although I agreed with him, was to sit down and cry. I felt very far from home and hopelessly inadequate in the preparation of mutton. The two other families on the farm were Dutch emigrants. They were friendly but our conversation was limited because of the language difference.

One of our first needs was to have transport, so we bought a very ancient navy blue Austin pick-up. It burned a lot of oil but did no-one any harm; it bumped its way easily over the stoned roads. The nearest town of Deloraine was ten miles away. We could all squeeze into the front, or one of us brave the empty back, clutching a child. On our days off we saw various parts of Tasmania; we visited the Great Lakes and a steep waterfalled ravine where the only snake I saw during our time there slithered gently and harmlessly across my path. There was very little traffic on the unmade roads; in all our travels we encountered practically no other vehicles.

We were a rarity in owning a car. One of our first tasks was to be present at the house of the old manager while his family waited at his bedside for his death. I asked why it was necessary to wake the two children in the night for me to bring them to this auspicious occasion. The reason was that all the families were to be present, also our vehicle, the only motorised one except a tractor, might be needed to fetch the doctor.

I soon got to know the owners of the local shop in the small collection of houses called Chudleigh. We bought all our groceries there. It was owned by an English couple with a grown-up daughter. They had first come out from England to Tasmania a number of years before. In fact they had settled nowhere, returning to England twice and then unable to settle there, had returned to Tasmania. This process they were hoping to repeat once again for the third time. It was a case of perpetual yearning for whichever life they were not in — I dreaded to become like this. Divided loyalties would be too hard to live with. Many emigrants living in Australia longed for home. When at home they missed

Jim, Kenneth and Robert in the 'bush'

something of Australia, the climate, the more classless society or their friends. We were invited to Christmas dinner with the family. Behind the shop were the living quarters. The Christmas pudding was served and we all sat round the table in the heat to celebrate. The buzzing of the flies were the chorus to the occasion, unnoticed by all I am sure, but Jim and myself. I have frequently thought since what a boon to the world the manufacture of flykiller has been and I see again that Christmas dinner in the back room of the shop at Chudleigh.

Jim worked hard and the children grew into sturdy little boys. Robert could nearly walk when the Manager decided to move us to another house on the estate called Rock Fields. The white, simple, four-roomed stone house was a settler's farmhouse. The barn opposite was a magnificent stone building with hay racks, mistals and stabling, an empty monument to what the farm had once been. A veranda and a kitchen had been added to the original house. The wild garden surrounding it was full of damson trees. Wombatts walked along the tin roof at night and seemed to be our only companions. Jim now had to walk two miles back across a river and through paddocks to work. I could drive out a distance of three miles on a track across acres of ploughed land to Chudleigh.

One evening the owners of the shop decided to show us an empty farm just past the little tin-roofed houses — perhaps we would be interested in buying it. The small three-roomed wooden house was set a few hundred yards back from the road. The greater portion of the land was arable and was fenced against rabbits, in large square paddocks, out of sight some 200 feet higher than the tussocked thistle and gorse infested land surrounding the house. It was, Jim told me, lovely land, suitable for growing corn and would be fertile to farm. The next evening we visited the neighbouring farmer. The owner was a young Australian who was married to an English girl from the Northumberland area. We drove up the steep hillside until we were level with the top land of the farm which was for sale. Here the grass was completely eaten away by rabbits. The place was alive with them running in every direction. The young mother was bathing her baby in a tin bath on the floor of the one roomed wooden hut that was their home. Sadly she told us that they had no grass to feed anything; all her husband could do was to snare hundreds of rabbits a day. They had no money and very little prospect of ever making anything of the farm. As for going home to England, how was she ever to get the money for the fare?

We had to decide whether we should try and buy the farm outside Chudleigh. It might be sold cheaply but the house was not in a very weatherproof condition. This time it was my turn to say 'No, I am going back to England and taking the children. If you do not come I will go alone'. I knew that if Jim refused to come with me I would find it impossible to go alone. Luckily Jim decided he would come too. We had lived cheaply on the estate and earned enough money to buy our tickets home. It was not the life or country I wanted to settle in for good

... AND HOME AGAIN

In letters from England we received a newspaper cutting stating that High Woods Farm was again on the market. With a great longing to be back home I telegraphed Uncle, asking him to buy the farm for us again. Our money was still under his guardianship at home as in 1950 no-one could take more than £15 with them out of England. A small amount even in those days to set up home again! Once more we packed up our things and set out for Hobart in the pick-up. Here luck was with us, a small cargo boat was in the harbour loading for departure in a few days time. It was to be the *San Georgio's* last trip before breaking. 'Do you dare to take your wife and family on that rusty heap of steel?' said the harbourmaster to Jim, and we both answered 'yes'. A few days later as the engines roared and shuddered into action, and a cloud of soot fell from the funnel on to our unsuspecting heads, we set out on a most interesting eight weeks journey home.

Next to our cabin on the deck was the cabin of an Italian doctor. He looked dubiously at us and the children, saying that he liked quiet. Ken was a notoriously early riser and would jump about over the bunks and was very hard to silence. Jim soon had an idea for them. Every morning he, Robert and Ken went out on to the deck and to the amusement of the sailors, helped them to wash the decks with mops and buckets. I washed the clothes and hung them out in the cabin to dry. The simple meals were served with cafe au lait, to Italian music from the loudspeaker on the deck. For weeks afterwards the small selection of songs were ingrained into my mind. We crossed the Indian Ocean, standing in the bow of the ship, ropes at our feet, we were in contact with the sea — as we dipped down the spray and warm air touched our faces. At night the stars of the Southern Hemisphere lit the sky — we were in touch with the oceans as we had never been in the *Orcades*.

Our first port of call was Colombo where we stopped for several days. The derricks were kept busy swinging bales of rubber into the hold. We were already well down into the sea when we took on 200 Indians who also lived in the hold. The conditions must have been terrible with the sound of the engines, the smell of the rubber and the heat of the tropics. They never appeared on deck or came up into daylight for food. They were confined to the hold for several days until we reached Massawa on the shores of the Red Sea on the East African coast. The Indians disembarked to seek the jobs they had come to find in Africa, and again cargo was taken on and off. The heat was so intense that only Jim, from our family, could face a walk on shore. The journey took us around the Cape of Good Hope and eventually into the Mediterranean and on to Venice.

The small ship edged its gentle way into the harbour on a calm misty morning. The green walled buildings, wharfs and waterways lapped by the sea, looked in some cases perilously near collapse, hiding as they did the magnificence of Venice which we were yet to see. We walked amongst the pigeons in St Peter's Square and took a trip on a gondola before leaving the harbour.

Once again the ship was guided out of the myriad of waterways by the pilot boat, the lighthouse was passed and we were on the last stage of our journey to arrive at Brindisi. We took the train in the late afternoon, sitting amongst the local farmers, who were going home after market day.

Happy and voluble, a farmer's wife sat smilingly beside us with a basket full of eggs. The train took us to Milan where we were to catch the night express to Paris and Calais. Darkness fell as we boarded the express which, as far back as 1952, did a speed of 180 mph. Ken and Robert lay across our knees fast asleep and oblivious of the countries through which they travelled. We passed Lake Geneva, surrounded by lights which shone out over the silver water. By daylight we had reached France and the train sped by white farm houses and lush green meadows.

Now almost at the end our our journey we were soon aboard the ferry to reach Dover in the afternoon. As we stood on the platform at Kings Cross I racked my brain for Al's telephone number. It came to me in a flash although I had never been able to remember if before or since! After a good night's sleep we were on our way north. How good it was to be home.

BACK TO HIGH WOODS

We returned to High Woods by train and quickly settled in. My Aunt had bought us a bed with a mahogany head and footboard, also some chairs and a table. They had come from an expensive shop in Scarborough; we felt a little less grateful when, a few weeks later, we received the bill. As the years pass and I see the modern beds I am increasingly pleased to own it and remember our first sight of our lovely furniture, which is still in use.

Electricity had still not come to Nidderdale and water was still unpiped. A huge brick settling-tank had been built but it did no good towards purification of the water or gaining a license to sell milk. Our trunks were unpacked and the primus and blankets were once again in use. The water still had to be pumped to the tank above by hand. Standing by the sink pumping the handle hundreds of times I began to realise the folly of thinking one can ever go back, it cannot be done, one must always go forward.

We settled down to rearing calves but on such a small acreage the money earned was not sufficient for a good living. David, our third son, was born and Ken was nearly five and would have to start school. Again it seemed only sensible to sell up and get somewhere more accessible and with better prospects. We moved to Doncaster and lived in a bungalow beside the main London to Edinburgh railway line. Ken started at a school only a few minutes walk away. Nothing could have been a bigger contrast to the Dales than the flat waste lands behind Bessacar stretching beside us to the outskirts of the west of the town. The fast trains sped past the side of our garden. Many of the engine drivers gave us a cheerful wave if the signals were against them, slowing them down to wait and belch out smoke. At the other side of the crossing lived an old man in an ancient railway coach. He kept goats — they seemed my only link with the countryside. Jim took his Ferguson tractor with him and started taking any contract work that he could find. Times however were changing and very many of the farmers who would have had their tractor work done for them only a few years previously had now bought their own tractors. When work was found and completed it was amazing how many farmers would be away for the day when Jim went for the money owing. One, it turned out, had even sold the farm and gone to America never to return to pay us at all.

One day we saw an advertisement Sturton Mill for Sale in Lincolnshire. The cottage was only £1000 if the new owner would undertake to work in the mill in the next village. The cottage had a good garden, orchard and buildings. The old mill with it, although no longer working, was in quite good repair making a useful shed. We decided to buy and now we had a roadside gate, electricity, mains water and eventually, when Tessa was born, a washing machine! Many of the fields were ploughed land which looked stunning stretching across to the Wolds.

Lincolnshire is a county of wide horizons — if the skies are

Sturton Mill, 1958. With David in front

Sturton Mill as it was

grey, unlike Yorkshire, it does not always mean rain. We seemed as if we might have everything. Jim never regretted giving up working for himself and worked in two industries before retirement. He worked at the mill and then some months later went to an agricultural engineering firm. One day he was working near the railway line and a man climbed up the bank towards him and asked him if he would go to work on the railways as they needed men who could work alone and were reliable. So it was that he started working on the railways as a linesman, later becoming a porter and then training as a signalman.

Ken and Robert went to the village school and in 1956 Tessa was born. Two years later David joined Ken and Robert at school and settled down happily. At this time Dr Beeching was asked by the Government to reconstruct the railways in a more viable way. The result was that many jobs were axed, small stations and signal boxes were closed. Jim lost his job and was told he could get a job at Starbeck in Harrogate. We decided we should move there to keep in employment. We would again be in Yorkshire and prospects seemed good.

Mill House, Sturton by Stow, Lincolnshire. 1954

HARROGATE

We sold the mill at Sturton and moved into a semi-detached house in Harrogate. Our small dinghy and trailer came in useful to carry extra tools and ladder. We had not been in our new home long when the next door neighbour said I have not worked all my life to retire into a bungalow only to find four children and a boat loaded with rubbish moving in next door; He put up with it for the next 3 years while we lived there.

The children went to a school nearby — not a happy school for David who seemed to be victimised from the very start, an experience he told me 40 years later, that had affected his liking for school for the rest of his life. Ken loved it there and decided we had ruined his life when we left. Robert accepted it all in stoic silence. Tessa was still a baby and enjoyed going about in the battered pushchair and playing in the sunny bright house.

When Jim went for his railway job at Starbeck signalbox he found that it too had been closed. He found work in a garage until another job was found at Poole in Wharfdale as porter on the station. Eventually we began to wish for a country life again with more scope. Jim moved once again to a signalbox at Horsforth when Poole station was closed. We looked around for a small farm nearer the job. Selling our house we just managed to buy our present home, Hardwick House Farm. No-one else wanted it, the prospect of living there dismayed many but we have managed to improve and enjoy living there.

TWENTY SEVEN LESS FAVOURED ACRES

When we arrived at the farm we were given some help and dire warnings. You must mind the stone gatepost in the top field, it once fell on someone. I give it a friendly pat as I pass it, it still leans but seems safe for a few more years — whoever put it back did a good job. 'A man was killed in the back field, he fell off a hay cart'. It is a nice field to walk in.

When I first visited the farm the fog was so thick nothing could be seen beyond the fields but I went home to report to Jim that it was a lovely little farm, and that we should buy it. Later, with my heart having ruled my head to such an extent, it was lucky that a nuclear power station was not just beyond the boundary. The house, nestling into the moorside, was built of solid stone with a slate roof. It had a bathroom, electricity and a telephone which Tessa, then aged four, liked very much. The barn was built with thick oak beams smoothed by an adze, made out of great tree trunks. Our neighbour's rams were peacefully sleeping behind a low oak door which led to the cow standings. When we turned them out they butted each others horns all night under our bedroom window. 'I hope you are not living in sin' was another remark. 'What with four children?' I exclaimed when I heard what had been said! So with the warning 'You should not be working on a Sunday' we smiled to ourselves and carried on as those people from Doncaster, a misunderstanding, as Jim had never lived in the town but in the pit villages and on the farms around the South Yorkshire area. For myself, I did not know where I was from — was I a child from Hackney, London, a girl from Birmingham, or the teenager cycling around the lanes of Hertfordshire?

We arrived at hay time in 1960, and as was the custom with Dales farmers, our nearest farming neighbours kindly offered to cut and turn our hay. We all put it into haycocks with two-pronged forks and wooden rakes. Eventually the hay was fit to be led into the barn adjoining the house, by tractor and trailer, where it was piled up to reach the beams. The beautiful smell of new mown hay permeated throughout the whole house and was remarked on by any of our relations or friends who came to stay. Today with silage and big bales the real essence of hay-making has been lost.

The road into our farm was stoned practically all of its two miles when we moved in. If every gate was shut it meant nine gates had to be opened but luckily this was rarely the case. We have managed to remove several by now and have a cattle grid at our entrance. We have put many tons of stone on the road to enable it to take the vehicles of today. Originally it was little more than a track leading from the entrance, between the fields, through the yards and on down to Ilkley. In days gone by it was used by local farmers. Now the path takes many hiking feet. Twice a council road was proposed but was turned down. Agreement could not be reached as a council road had to be fenced off by each farmer and those with more land had to spend more. Those with less would get their road for less, and that would never do! Now we might be tempted to think about the lack of foresight as properties would have been worth more and transport easier but something unique would have been lost, the tranquillity. With a beautiful view across the valley, seen under ever changing light and skies, we settled in to start a life of get-ting out to work' and 'down to school' in all weathers. With yet another warning from Jim's father 'You cannot live on a view', I said to myself '...but it helps ..' Sadly he died before he could come again. Jim's mother came often until she died at ninety. The first thing we did after we had settled in was to improve the water supply which ran down from the moors in an open channel in the neighbouring field. After a storm, grass and soil would wash down the moorside and in drought the main stream was lost amongst crannies and moss. It was now the era of plastic, the alkathene pipe had arrived, with the easily assembled connec-tions, the whole job was made easy. It was mainly a case of time, so Jim chose his summer holiday to start work. Coinciding with school holidays his four labourers were at the ready. Ken, now 14 was the map maker, the little diagram of the water course from the spring 400 yards above, ran down the wallside to our main header tank in the field. The moor is at its best in the summer. The sun brings out all the scent of decaying heather and bracken beneath, and the warmth rises around you giving a delicious feel-ing of wellbeing. No wonder sheep like to amble amongst rock and bilberry or lie contentedly chewing, surveying the hillside around, while pipits flit from rock to rock twittering and feeding. All went well and by the end of the week the job was completed and has only needed slight attention twice since.

Water was now plentiful, running from the overflow to rejoin the stream a few yards further on and thence on to the stream which watered stock on its journey down to the Wharfe. It was the little pools and rocks that the water gathered round whilst it remained on our land that gave us the idea of making several ponds, each one to overflow and feed into the next down the hill-side. Jim was in his element ditching or landscaping and soon produced a square fishpond. We stocked it with 8 Rudd and a Dace, a pale replica of the golden coloured Rudd. They swam in a shoal, turning and darting to their hearts content. As time went by we noticed their number decreasing, then even the Dace disappeared and only 2 of the Rudd were left. Eventually early one morning we saw the culprit, a Heron perched on a half stake beside the water. We had discovered that a pond cannot be without a net. True wilderness was gone for ever. We made a new pond further down the garden and put a net over it, re-stocking with a few more Rudd and Golden Orf. We soon found that Goldfish from the fair could not withstand the extreme cold or the acidity of the water. Koi carp did live well, and many have lived on to ages of 15 or more years and with a few additions we have kept the numbers up to about 40 beautiful fish, seen to their best advantage when the sun is directly above, slanting down through the clear water on a summer morning. So the garden developed, not into a professionally paved, expensively stocked area, but a quiet sunny corner to have coffee in.

When we first arrived we brought our small wooden green-house with us. The winds could be very strong on the moorside and although it was put up in a sheltered corner the gales took their toll, and one year smashed all the glass. Jim measured up and ordered new glass which he and David set out to collect one Saturday. Carefully packed in the back of the car they arrived home, and so started one of the best 'do you remember when I ' tales. David, then aged about 10, ran round to the back of the car, and in sandals and grey shorts jumped in on top of the covered glass, all eagerness to be of help. Absolute horror overtook the onlookers. Jim lifted him out, took the old groundsheet off the top and every piece of glass which had been skillfully cut by Mr Titmarsh was smashed. Not one word was spoken in reprimand. David ran upstairs to sit on his bed. A few minutes later Tessa went up to sympathise and then we all sat down for dinner, a little chastened. Next weekend the glass was ordered again and fetched; and with a 'don't jump in this time David' all went well. The greenhouse continued life for another 10 years. Eventually the gales wrecked it all again. David, who was then married and living in llkley, took it down to his more sheltered garden and rebuilt it, giving it an up-to-date sliding door. It remains there today, as I have always thought, in the very best hands.

The house was once described by one of the many walkers who pass through the yard 'nowt but a cottage'. It is built of stone hewn out of the quarry which was once dominant behind us on the moorside. Our six small fields were chosen as the tipping area for most of the waste soil and small stones that were laid down from the quarry. The hillocks and hollows are a variant of all shales, sands and clays that can be imagined. On the turf that has grown over it the sheep and calves live happily. Before hay was bought in we were practically weed free. Unfortunately this is far from true now. All the corners of the fields from which grass has been made into hay have deposited hundreds and thousands of weed seeds, dock, nettles and thistles. There are advantages in this. I have been able to watch ten goldfinch feeding on the thistle seeds under my kitchen window all the week.

The house stands four square and sheltered from the westerly wind by the largest hillock upon which there are three horse chestnut trees. It is a friendly house. I have been out on many occasions at night to visit the lambing shed, exercise the dogs or look for predicted stars or northern lights, without the slightest feeling of unease. There are no ghosts here.

Jim and his mother and father had a different tale to tell of a house which they moved into when he was about 10 years old. I have no hesitation in believing the ghosts were there and that the happenings were exactly as told. The house was a colliery house, one in a long street of houses, but this one had been empty for a long time. Mother and Jim moved in with their few bits of furniture, clipping rugs and crockery. Dad had to go on the night shift at the pit and had not been able to help with the move. As they settled down to an evening beside the newly lit fire and candlelight, the electricity had not yet been re-connected, they sat, one each side of the fire, Jim in an arm chair and Mother on a one ended settee. All at once one of the kitchen chairs slowly rose from the floor and hovered at the ceiling for several seconds before landing again on the floor with a clatter. 'Did you see that Mum?' Jim said to his mother. 'Yes' she replied, 'perhaps your Dad is wondering if we are alright'. The next night as Dad lay in bed an unseen force fought with him as he ran down the stairs. Jim slept with the blankets well· over his head. Three days later they were allocated a different house in the long street named 'Broadway'. The worst of it was all the bedding had to be burned for as well as being haunted the house was infested with bugs. The family never heard what strange happenings had caused the haunting.

Our house was, however, very ordinary and comfortable. One of the main beams has always been a great source of interest to previous owners who have returned to the barn to see if it is still 'alright'. I am sorry to disappoint them but it probably has more strength than any new house beam. Another huge oak beam goes through the main bedroom and bathroom. Eventually after many years I finally got rid of the layers of wallpaper which were on the walls. I did not get down to the staircase until David had left home and was visiting us with his wife Sandra. We were discussing the untidiness of the paper on the stairs. 'Oh, that's easy, I'll soon get that off' said David, and he took hold of the nearest corner of loose paper and pulled. An hour later he stood victorious amongst a pile of multi-coloured papers and lime flakes which were strewn across the corner of the living room from where the stair door opens. 'I am afraid I've got to go home now' he said. Many times since then I have thought with amusement of the way he got me into tackling the stairs.

Our first Autumn we knew nothing much of the house, the

land or the winters. I would walk down the fields with our three boys, who had already had several years of school and Tessa who was just starting. Four fields below us we met three other children. Leaving boots in the farm buildings for the return trip, they put their shoes on and got into the school taxi for the 3 mile journey to a central pick-up point at the infants' school. Although it could be cold with driving icy rain or sleet in the face, there was and still is, nothing to do but put the head down and battle on. Compensations were, however, many. I can remember standing at a small clump of alder trees, waiting. November snow was falling. In its damp clinging state the snow was building up on every branch and wall in an amazingly quick and supremely silent way. The sky behind the trees was indigo. Suddenly through the flakes, flying low, came the V formation of geese calling as they went. If I do not see a skein of geese at least once in the Autumn I feel I have missed something very important. Perhaps the primeval signs of winter or weather to come still urge us to take heed. This year we were lucky to see forty in two formations calling as they went.

For most of our school years we had a much loved companion, a labrador-cross bitch, black with a white star on her chest. She had come into our household when Jim had finally left the job on the railways, with the closure of the Horsforth signal box. He started work on the water board in the all important filtration department. One night he was sitting waiting for his pay in a room at the depot when a young man came in with his black dog. As he went by he asked Jim if he could just look after his dog for a minute. Bess sat down in front of Jim, gazing up at him with her brown faithful eyes. When the man returned he told Jim he was on his way to have the dog put down. She was only nine months old but she 'had not a brain in her head'. 'No need to do that', Jim replied, 'I'll have her'. Bess lived contentedly with us and us with her for seventeen years. She just managed to live until all the children had left home. She began to fail shortly before Tessa's wedding day. For her own sake we put her in the barn while the wedding reception took place. At the very end of the day as Ken departed for home he said to his Dad, 'You cannot leave Bess in the barn, go and fetch her in'. This Jim tried to do, but she growled and begged to be left alone in the place that all the dogs have loved. In the morning a faithful friend had died.

By 1963 we thought we were quite good at preparing for winter. With no freezers it was a case of stocking up with tins, flour and sugar, coal and logs and hoping that the snow did not last long. There would be a holiday from school as long as the roads were blocked. Jim managed to walk down to his job during most of the snowy times in winter. Any stock we had, generally only a few cows or calves, were housed in the barn. They had a contented few months. For the sheep it is a different story. Lying against the walls in the lea of the wind, they wait frozen and snow covered until I am in sight with a bale of hay. I try to make sure they are in fields near to the buildings, as it is hard work searching and climbing amongst the rocks and heather in snow. Like the Kestrel that has for the many years roosted during winter on the waste pipe from the bathroom, I like to feel the shelter of the buildings behind me.

Eventually it became necessary to 'turn' the slates on the roof of the house, renew any necessary timbers and lay roofing felt. We had been fortunate in always having an expert roofing firm only a mile away; although the friendly drip over our bed, by which we could judge the wildness of a storm had never been cured. Eventually we were told that the the time had come for the timbers to be built up and the slates to be 'turned'. The Autumn was the best time to do it. Two weeks before Christmas the men arrived. 'Yes, it would be done before Christmas' and they set to work placing the slates upright along the ridge. Forty tons of slate was propped up above us. We hoped for fine weather. New pieces of wood were hammered into place, the felt was laid and the slates were 'turned'. Christmas week arrived and the job was all but done. The builder came down from the roof and I went out and stood beside him in the back field looking up. 'What do you think of it now? I said. With a glowing face he replied 'I think it's marvellous'. 'And so do I' I answered. What a satisfying job it must be to see your craft, cold, heavy and exacting, but so beautifully enhancing the countryside. The men went away for Christmas but that was not quite the end of the story. The scaffolding was left up to finish off the replacing of the coping stones. The day after Christmas a blizzard blew up. A tremendous clatter in the night indicated something — in the morning we saw it had blown down the scaffolding, narrowly missing the window and a gate. As we urged the frozen cows into shelter we stood looking across at the house through the blinding snow. After the holiday everything returned to normal and the workmen returned and retrieved the scaffolding and finished the job. It had all gone well. Snow no longer blows under the slates to melt and make damp patches on the ceiling. It all looks just perfect. When Spring came the bats flew out as usual; they had not been disturbed in the least. It is a sobering thought however, that the cost of the roof was one and a half times more than the cost of the farm had been in 1960. The barn looks just a little more uneven. A thin layer of snow can still blow under the slates, to cover every ledge, bin, bag or bale. It might last out until the present 'peasant in the cottage' has gone, and, like so many small attractive buildings, is forced into the twenty first century to be made into a 'residence for a lady'.

Spring eventually comes, even though at times it feels as if it never will. One morning the sun feels warm on your shoulders and head and you gaze about in amazement saying 'the sun really feels warm'. After many years experience I have learned that this means little, and there are many days to come before it is safe to wash your gloves and put them away until next winter. Gradually the light evenings become warm evenings.

One summer morning I walked the 20 yards from the back door to the moor gate and a beautiful roe deer was feeding contentedly on the other side. Only trying to alert Jim to come and see it sent it off up the moor at great speed. Three times we have had deer close to the house. Strictly, I suppose they are not really wild but have escaped from estates to live as best they can. Several are always in the reservoir grounds. One lived for a winter in the shelter of woods by the river. As new grass grew it was tempted to come across the main road and up the fields below us to arrive at the field behind the house. Finding ewes and lambs there, they all started circling around chasing each other. I was tempted to go out with a camera, and the speed of retreat back down to the woods, taking walls, fences and wires with elegant and faultless exactness, needed to be seen to be believed.

The two other creatures which are always here are the fox and the badger. One summer night Jim put on the kitchen light and it shone out to light up a family of badgers feeding just outside the window. Foxes also regularly can be heard giving their eerie bark as dusk comes. Occasionally they can be seen slinking by on whatever errand they are about. It is hoped, not one to the hen-house. If ever the hens are left out they will be missing by morning. If a lamb is missing and cannot be found the fox is always blamed.

Many friends and relations visited us in the summer. Al and Jen came to the north at some time during her school holidays. Jen was between Ken and Robert in age. People are wont to say that it 'must be nice to live on a permanent holiday!' One summer a Swedish boy came to stay. He was from an intellectual family; his mother was a psychologist, his father worked as a translator. Per wanted to be a surgeon. They lived in a flat in Stockholm. The first morning after his arrival, the older boys went out and climbed a wall — a stone fell on Per's hand. We saw at once that a hospital visit was necessary. This fair, serious boy, was very upset — how could his hand be mended well enough in a small English town to enable him to still become a surgeon? His hand was put in plaster in the local hospital and all went well. After his return home his Swedish doctor wrote both to us and to the hospital thanking us for looking after Per so well; he would still be able to become a surgeon which eventually he did! The handicapped hand did little to spoil Per's holiday. It was fascinating to watch the sixteen year old, who had never had much opportunity to play, becoming more like our fifteen and thirteen year old. I thought the metamorphosis was complete when I saw him trying to drag Ken and Robert to the pond to dump them in it. When Per returned to Sweden Ken went on a return visit. He safely reached home again having had an interesting holiday. It was the beginning of his many journeys to all parts of Europe as coach driver in his travel firm.

I do not know if we can be said to be privileged or cursed to have received a notification that our moor is now a SSSI, that means a 'Site of Special Scientific Interest' which now extends across all the South Pennines. One thing I learned from the SSSI is that the little birds that twitter on the moor amongst the heather and bilberry are Twite not Pipits which I thought they were, but are they right? Do any of them know their birds? I will just have a peep in the Handbook later on when no one is looking to make sure.

To us at the farm the Moor holds a very personal pleasure. Apart from its population of upland birds which vary with the seasons, it now has upwards of two hundred trees. We have planted many trees and shrubs to encourage birds and animals and to shelter the exposed hillside which surrounds the house. The Mountain Ash, Birch and English Ash have spread far and wide. The seeds are carried by bird or wind, and young trees are growing everywhere in sheltered crannies. Each year one or two more appear. Sheltered for their first few years by the height of the bracken they seem to survive the grazing sheep and suddenly appear tall and strong dotted amongst the rocks and bilberry. Some trees have gone. A giant hawthorn in front of the house used to hold a swing which was made out of a rope and tyre. One wild morning I saw Jim off to work. It was pitch dark as I walked back to the house, the wind gusted and the whole ground seemed to shudder. When daylight came I could see what had happened, the tree had gone. The great mass of roots had been uprooted from the ground. The branches lay in a tangled mass of gnarled sharp twigs. It took a long time and strong gloves for us to clear it into manageable pieces for the fire. In its place we planted a maple — one of our regular walkers of the footpath said to Jim 'At any rate you will be remembered for your trees' — what better epitaph could there be.

With the aid of agricultural grants we have managed to fence the wall-tops to keep out persistent sheep following their ancestors with an ability to cross any boundary. Most can be kept from the forbidden land. As the bracken grows it seems to protect the slender stems of the trees from a small number of sheep, mainly grazing in the Autumn when the growing season is over. Our small flock love to go up to the heather tops as dusk falls. The SSSI officials, along with the Wheatear and the Twite, also have a growing miniature forest on their protected land of sixteen acres, part of a vast area of the Pennines which stretches as far as South Derbyshire.

New Zealand

In 1972 Jim thought he would, as it is called today, take six months 'out from his job' and have a trip to New Zealand. This time he would fly out via Los Angeles to Auckland. On a foggy October morning I drove him to Yeadon Airport for the first stage of his journey. Perhaps no planes would fly? Jim was determined to see New Zealand which we had not done in 1951 when in Autstralia. Three days later he had arrived in Gisbourne, New Zealand and found somewhere to stay. He arranged a train and bus tour of the two islands. On returning to Gisborne he decided to get a job and was able to rent a bungalow in the Maori area of the town. Jim went to the Water Board and asked for a job, any job. No, he didn't mind getting his hands dirty. When he returned next morning the boss said they wanted him to work for the Water Department and read meters throughout the area. He was to take a fortnight in the office learning where every street was and then take the van and start the job.

Jim went to many places in his free time and lived contentedly amongst the Maoris. His neighbour left a bag of carrots on his doorstep in exchange for the mending of his lawnmower.

March came round and I wondered if he could leave it all to

come home. I knew his return ticket would be running out in April. Tessa and I were tired of living on our own. The winter had been a mild one and we had managed to drive out every day to get her to the bus for college to study child care at Bradford. One night the phone rang and we ran downstairs to answer it. Jim was ringing from the Post Office in Gisborne, he would be home in three days time.

Al

In the mid seventies Al was ill and told us she was to have an operation. We all thought this would be quite straightforward. A few days later she rang us from the hospital — she was distraught. The Sister had come to her while she was having her dinner to tell her she had cancer and nothing could be done. Jim and I told her we would come on the early train from Leeds to be with her at visiting time the next day. She did not want to come to stay with us as she was loath to leave home and Jen, who was living within reach, with her husband Charlie. She went through the chemotheraphy while staying with Bill Miall, of our teenage years and his wife, who lived at Jordans in Buckinghamshire. Eventually she was well enough to return briefly to her job at school where she was now deputy head and to undertake a drive north to see us in the summer. It was a sunny warm spell of weather and she was full of hope that she would beat the illness and see her grandchildren grow up.

One afternoon we sat out on the flagstones eating chocolate cake when the man from the Ministry of Agriculture came to count our hill cows. He took a look at us sitting there and smiled broadly. I said 'yes, we are rather alike. This is my twin sister Al. Have some chocolate cake', and we all laughed. He had visited us for nearly twenty years, once a year since and I have never known his name. Sometimes when his car pulls into the yard I remember that summer day nearly twenty years ago. One of Al's favourite places was Malham Tarn which we visited on her last visit. We parked the car and walked over the springy grass towards the waters edge. Looking down the grass was full of wild pansies, yellow and purple. 'Heartsease it is called' I thought to myself, 'and will they ease the heart?'

A few months later I went down to stay with Al. She had to give up work at school but she was still absolutely determined to get better. When I arrived she asked me where I was going to sleep. 'Why here' I said, 'on this little divan in here with you. We can talk late into the night as we did when we were children'. One night she said to me in the darkness 'Do you remember when I threw the bedside light at you?' I replied that I certainly did and 'I still have the mark to show for it'. I believe she had been getting up in the darkness to give me a good thump for something I had said or done. It was so long ago I could not remember what, but I knew the lamp had fallen accidentally. 'Do you remember how we used to hold hands between the beds as we fell asleep' I said, and she did remember.

A few days later Jen and I got up and Al told us she had arranged by telephone to go back into hospital. It was time for me to go home. I caught the London train to Leeds with a heavy heart and tears not far away. We rushed past the fields and through the stations. The passengers silently engrossed in their papers or their thoughts. When we reached Wakefield, the doors flew open, people got out and the Yorkshire folk got in. The whole atmosphere changed, everyone started to laugh and talk. It is a phenomenon I have noticed many times since that day. It feels as if the grey haired grandmas are about to fling their arms about you, so like Mother are they in looks and voice. The Dads heave their suitcases on to the racks and sit down with a happy sigh. Once again Yorkshire people envelope you and you feel at home. But I have never felt so cheered as I did that first time I experienced it.

A fortnight later Charlie, Jen's husband, rang me to say that Al had died. It is a strange thing that it seems as if she has never really left us. I sometimes still talk more like her than myself, but then Jim could never tell which of us was talking if we were in a different room from him.

While I was staying with Al, shortly before she died, a friend visited her. I remember going up to her bedroom. Al was sat gaunt in her blue dressing gown. The friend was trying to persuade her to discuss her funeral. 'You can do what you like' she said 'I am not interested'. 'Isn't it time you went home?' I said to the friend. In the event we all went down in our cars to Watford Crematorium where Jen had decided on a Quaker service. The room was filled with Al's friends and relations. As is the custom at a Quaker funeral anyone moved to speak can get up and do so, as in a meeting for worship. Many lovely and kind things were said. On the way out, seeming quite alone, I looked down where the flowers had been flung on a flight of cement steps. The rain was falling heavily by now, all the messages were smudged. Thinking that it was no good to try to read them I turned away to find Leonard was standing beside me. He was so like my Uncle, the years fell away and I was reminded of our years at Sewells Orchard. We chatted about our families and our doings. I remembered my Aunt, and how she had once said that 'Al was like a young gazelle as she had jumped up in her cotton dress, from the hearth rug, lithe and graceful'. We had laughed at the description in the sunny sitting room at Sewells Orchard. I went on to talk with Nan, and my cousin Margaret, who was shepherding my Birmingham Uncle Wilfrid and Aunt Winifred, now bent and in their late eighties, but still strong and interested in all that was going on around them.

Eventually we were back in Al's house. As we drank our coffee and ate our sandwiches, James, Al's first grandchild aged two, clutched at my skirt. I thought how sad it was that she had not been able to take him round the new Lake they had built in Welwyn, to feed the ducks, as she had planned.

A few months later Jen, Charlie, James and baby Nicola moved into Al's house. Ben was born two years later and the house and garden was full of the sound of a family again.

Now as they start to go out into the world of work and marriage, three young people are about to embark on their own life stories.

Al would have been proud of her grandchildren.

The Fourteen Gated Road

When my son Robert and his family come to stay we generally take a trip out to some part of the Dales. Although it is more peopled than when we first visited around 1938, it is still a unique part of the world. Malham is still a favourite place to visit. Travelling down from Addingham to Bolton Abbey is one of the most beautiful stretches of land, following as it does the River Wharfe, with woods and hills rising to the higher fells above. Turning left after reaching Kilnsey, the River Skirfare flows down from the limestone countryside of Littondale. It is a twisting but lovely drive up the dale to Halton Gill. Here the road turns left and rises steeply and magnificently then drops sharply to the valley and river below. In front of you are Pen-y-ghent and Ingleborough with Whemside behind. The famous three peaks.

On one of our trips this way I suddenly realised that this was indeed the fourteen-gate road of my youth. I remembered being driven along here by my Uncle in the old fashioned Austin car. Alice and I rode on either side standing on the running board, waiting to leap off in turn at each of the fourteen gates to swing them open.

Sure enough as we counted, the wheels rumbled over the thirteen cattle grids. The remaining gate was at Darnbrook House Farm. Here the road dips steeply in either direction. In summer black hill cows and their calves lie out in the sun.

One winter day taking the same route we reached Kilnsey in brilliant February sunshine and were not even warned of a change in the weather by a huge black grey cloud to the west. On reaching Arncliffe and then on to Halton Gill, things had drastically changed. As we climbed up snow was falling fast, the view had gone and several inches of snow had fallen. Soon a snow plough was following us and there was no choice but to continue on down to Darnbrook and slowly up again. Eventually we crept down into Stainforth and Settle to sunshine with no snow on the verges or roads. On the higher Pennines the farmer and his family are really at the mercy of the weather.

The last calves we had on our farm were Galloways which had been reared on a high farm above Malham. We bought four black weaned calves straight off their mothers. I thought they would winter outside except in the very worst weather and that I could manage to look after them, perhaps getting them in calf and have the pleasure of these tough little beasts before I gave up farming completely. Galloways have, since the early years of farming, been no strangers to Malham. The old droving route from Scotland to the south east of England went along the ancient stone-walled grass routes of Malham Moor, south to Kent. The Galloway meat was well thought of then as it is today. The farmer was not in so much hurry to feed his beast, or in the position of being able to bring in manufactured foods from far away as they are today. If the farm only grew grass this was the feed. If it took three years to rear the animal this was taken and the meat was nicer as a result of fattening on grass.

When our little Galloways came down from 1000 feet to 800 feet they thought they had reached heaven. They started to eat their heads off. The first heifers were wild and although I wintered them inside in bitter snow or driving rain, I was never able to tie them up. They would eat in a friendly quiet way, but if they suspected a rope was about to be put round their necks they would whisk around and prefer to jump over the rail of their standing or flatten a moveable iron gate than to wait to see how harmless and comfortable being tied up was. I vowed that the next calves would be different. I would tie them from a week old when I really could hold them. I haltered and tied the two heifer calves which were born in the spring, during their first summer when I could. By the time they were old enough to have their own calves they were harder to keep out of the barn than to get in and ended up sleeping inside most of the winter. The older beasts had gone to market and I was left with the two daughters now both in calf. The decision had to be made — was it wiser to sell them or let them calve so that we could enjoy the calves and their mothers grazing in the field under the kitchen window? It seemed better to let them go now when they would make more money. I decided not to risk any mishaps at calving. New ear tagging and identification papers were coming, involving more work and expense for very little profit. The transport was arranged and the two heifers were loaded and taken to market. It was two years since I had been in the cattle market to sell their mothers. As I walked round the pens of cows and younger animals I was quite amazed to see how much older familiar faces looked. One of my near neighbours from whom I had bought young calves in earlier years nodded and spoke, momentarily I could not remember who he was, he looked so much older. Eventually my turn came, lots 43 and 44 were on their way into the ring. I quickly followed. The auctioneer I was used to was not in charge. He now had two young men, one in the cattle ring and one with him at the sheep pens. Handing over the details the auctioneer competently took the sale through. I tapped Crystal, the black heifer on her rump and around the ring she went. She then decided she would stop and look about, perhaps there would be a coat to chew or a fence to knock down? — two of her less endearing habits. She was sold, the gate clanged behind her and in came Ruby, the Hereford cross Galloway. Red and white, her brown eyes were a little reminiscent of her pure wild Galloway inheritance as she circled the ring at a quick run. No need to tap her. It would be hard to keep up, best to stand by and listen to the bidding. The selling was over and the sale had gone well. I had made £20 more than I had hoped for. On reaching the office to collect my money there were more signs of change. We had been modernised — the aristocratic bearded man who used to write out the cheques had been replaced by a girl and a computer. The sum was quickly tapped out, the cheque and bill of sale was twirled around, luck money was deducted and I was on my way home. My generation of farmers were soon to be replaced I reflected.

It would be rather nice without cows. Perhaps the fences would last my time out without Crystal. There would be more time to look after my sheep and for training my sheepdog. I would sit under the trees looking across our lovely valley more often.

CATS

We have had several cats while we have been on the farm, essential as they are for keeping mice and rats at bay. A tabby mother and son who were the first, lived seventeen years and fifteen. These two were followed by a tortoiseshell, who we were told 'must live in the house' as my daughter brought her from the car after her first camping trip with her cousin Jen. This was tried, but soon she was banished to the barn for a carefree life of her own.

Our next cat was a little grey waif that my grandsons Mark and Richard brought from their Auntie. She must live with us they said to avoid being run over by traffic. 'We can't have her at home'. I agreed with this, but wondered if this tiny scrap of life would live to see any traffic. Mark was nine and Richard six. The following weekend they brought a tin of cat food, 'We will feed it', they said, 'you won't have to do a thing'. The wisp, who never gained a name beyond that of 'kitten' continued to emerge from her hiding place behind bag or bale at regular intervals, luckily not absolutely dependant on her owners for food. The first tin was the last tin to be brought! Our not very friendly or sociable kitten was with us for about 13 years — we are not known for short-lived cats. Kitten's chief occupation had been sneezing on the windows, her working abilities were a little feeble and her friendship nil, except for being there. After she had gone rabbits seemed to be increasing, rats were also seen and I decided another cat would have to be found.

Summer holidays were here and two more of my grandchildren were staying with us. Peter was nine and Laura seven. We decided to go to our local corn mill and see if their beautiful tabby cat had kittens. The workers at the mill were delighted to find homes for the latest family. Dashing about they spent half an hour of hilarity finding two kittens from obscure comers of the buildings. A little ginger tabby who looked rather frail and a striped ginger kitten with white feet and front were chosen. Peter and Laura named them Mittens and Marmalade, two names which I secretly thought rather fanciful for working cats with a mill heritage. They never did become more than Tommy and Tabby to me. When we got home we shut them into the sheep shed and they grew and played and slept until they were over six months old. They looked so different from each other is was hard to believe that they were brother and sister. Tabby was a shy little female cat, while Tommy was twice her size, brave, beautiful and big. The morning of their release arrived. They had both been to the vet and they were free to roam their world. I thought they would understand that the sheep shed was their home. I was quite wrong, it took only the time to walk back to the barn adjoining the house for them to take up residence close to the back door into the house. They never went back to the sheep shed except to follow me down if I was working there, or to eat an occasional bird or rabbit under the warm sun slanting through the windows in the roof. By the time Tommy was 12 months old he hunted rabbits, catching them daily throughout the summer months. He roamed far and wide amongst the grasses and the brackens hunting or sleeping. Tabby was content with very small mice or voles until she was three, then she started to sit at rabbit holes and had occasional success carrying the odd rabbit home to the doorstep.

When I went to the sheep, beside the dog ran the two cats, faithfully following along the wall tops. If I was at the hen hut they sat on the tin roof above me. If I went to Tessa's cottage, three fields away, Tommy would follow and wait at the door or on the porch roof to escort me home.

Some time later, on a wet windy night, I realised that Tommy had not been sleeping in his dog basket or on their old sheepskin coat for several days or nights, nor had he been for food. Tabby was sitting on the windowsill, her ears pricked and twitching, her head turning to listen to every sound. She seemed to be straining every nerve to hear Tommy coming home. He did not appear and she slept alone. We enquired around, only to hear that two other cats had vanished. Perhaps shooting or poisoning had taken place and the cat had accidentally become prey to it. It is strange how bereft I feel without Tommy — his quick light step behind me on the wall top, making his presence known by the slight click of a rocking stone. Even in darkness his watchful presence was unseen beside me. There may be another Tommy but there will never be another Tommy Pearson from Pearsons' Mill. I miss my faithful feline follower.

WALKERS, AND TIME MARCHES ON ...

In the days when we first came to the farm people who walked on the footpath, which went directly past our windows, were few. A local farmer setting off to round up his sheep or a gamekeeper or neighbouring farmer's wife coming through 'to keep the footpath open' and have a gossip and a cup of tea, were the main people. We had two tramps, and then eventually one bearded figure in an old mac and laceless boots. He was a harmless soul who would travel through in one direction or the other about twice a year. My nearest neighbour, who had looked after him for years, would often give him something to eat or drink. If she was not in, he would knock at my door. He would sit on the stone steps of a building to eat his two boiled eggs, bread and tea. He was glad of a place where a meal could be obtained. Handing his cup and plate over, he would pass harmlessly on. Now in good weather we can get up to 100 people a week at a rough count. Regular clubs come through from Leeds or Bradford. Runners storing up hip troubles for the future pound by. Cyclists on mountain bikes are happy to lift their machines over the stiles and bowl over a stray hen as they rush by.

For a number of years we had a couple from Leeds who used to leave their car at the top of the lane and walk down to eat their lunch when they had reached our stile. They came every summer, looking at the improvements and alterations to the properties. If they could meet you at the gate they always talked of what they had seen. I was disappointed if a year went by and I had missed them. Eventually they must have become too old to drive or one or both had died and they ceased to come several years ago.

Some have been given nicknames such as 'the happy banker', a man who comes to a point just beyond our house to sadly gaze out over the beautiful evening valley once a week. Others have flamboyant clothes or gypsy-like clothes, they pass by eating a handful of berries which they have filched on the way through at dusk. I cannot leave out the autumnal mushroom pickers who generally seem 'high' before they even start cooking the 'happy mushrooms'. I have never discovered which are the ones they are after, but they go about bent double, gazing at the ground with their long hair draped about them, a white plastic bag in their hands. They have jumped all fences, walls or gates. It is safer not to accost them in any way. They think that it is 'God's free earth'. I am not sure which God they refer to but they certainly are sup-·porting the Government in the abandoning of the trespass law.

When Jim received the huge wage of £1000 a year, I thought we were affluent. I was sure we would never be wanting more money ever again. Of course it is all relevant to the times we live in. I am reminded of Mother who expressed the thought that the huge sum of £8 a fortnight that I spent on groceries should bring any grocery van rushing to my door, however isolated the place. We did have a grocery shop once which did exactly this. When I met the owner of the now defunct shop we started to discuss the work involved in shopping at supermarkets; he being now at least 80 and without transport. It was a very hard job, 'and to think' he said, 'we would go out with the van even on a demand for an ounce of yeast'. As Robert remarked to me when I was bemoaning the spending of £20 'You have to think of it in the terms of £20 being equivalent to one fill of a tank of petrol and it won't be missed'.

Very few of us today will ever be in the strait that Mother was in when Jim was a boy of about 12 in the thirties. Divine Intervention took a hand, or as I prefer to call it 'luck'. Every day that week Dad had gone out to work as usual to sign on each morning at the pit gates. As the mines were privately owned and there was no sale for coal at the time the men were sent home with no pay. The morning came when Mother had no money left in her purse and no bread in the cupboard. Suddenly a knock on the door surprised them. A workman stood there with a jug and tea leaves in his hand. He and his men were to be working across the road for the next week, would Mother supply them with boiling water to make their tea for a whole week. The man handed her five shillings. Mother protested that this was far too much money, she had coal for the fire to heat the free water. 'No love, I get paid for my work and you shall get paid for your work, take the money' he said. With tears in her eyes she thanked him and sent Jim off to buy a loaf. Breakfast was eaten after all that day.

So, our family have all grown up. Robert decided he liked farming quite early on in his life. David and Tessa were also happy to help us out in the fields if there was nothing more interesting going on. All the children learned the basics of driving our President tractor and enjoyed having ponies and calves. David went off daily to walk an old lady's dog — it was old too and quite happy to rest on a seat most of the time! Ken kept a few hens and made money by selling their eggs.

I still keep a few Rhodes and Light Sussex hens free range and it is surprising to find that this is the thing that people walking through enjoy looking at the most. It seems to be that it is very nostalgic!

Ken left home to do a business and accountancy course, Robert went away to Agricultural College, eventually becoming a teacher. David quickly followed in leaving school and with his practical skills joined the water industry.

In the early 1980s I started to keep a few sheep. They were Teeswaters mainly, a mixed bag of pet lambs from a nearby estate. I still think they are the breed Tessa and I like best. A particular one could easily have won a record if a proper tally had been kept of her lambs. We had her for over ten years and she had twins, several times she had triplets and one memorable occasion she had four lambs. All were reared, although not all by her. The last year she had lambs she had no teeth left and a week before she lambed she lay down to be fed where she lay. One evening I went out to the shed and she had two good lambs and was up walking about eating. The poor 'old lady' went out again into the fields and reared her lambs well. Clearly her time had come to be sold and in the autumn we reluctantly said 'goodbye' to 'Mrs Teeswater'. We have never had another quite like her. I then changed to a few Swaledales. We bought 20 and 19 lived a number of years and had good Suffolk cross lambs. Many of the ewe lambs are in the present flock. We often have lambs to bottle feed and last year 'Wilf and Wilma' were a great source of pleasure to my two youngest grand-daughters, who live close by with Tessa and Ian. The lambs enjoyed their bottles until the day they went. No one seemed to realise that their milk had turned to water with a dash of milk powder' in it for the cause of economic farming!

With sheep, of course the mind turns instantly to dogs. To me they are a great pleasure to have walking with you, the Border Collie particularly. Some I have managed to train to be a real help with the sheep, some have reluctantly had to be found other homes with more work and a more clever master. As with all things, it is the next thing you are going to do, and the next thing you will enjoy, which is important. Most enjoyable is watching our grandchildren grow up.

Recently Mark and Richard, now in the world of work, jumped from their car exclaiming 'It is all just the same'. We talked of their childhood den built on the moor and the cricket played against the barn door.

Lisa, Catherine and Rachel sit at the table to paint a picture of Meg, my border collie. She lies patiently waiting on the hearth rug until her portrait is finished.

Peter and Laura, home from school, come to fish in the pond for tadpoles. Their newly made pond at home needs frogs, snails and plants.

Seth and Ruth visit us. They hurry to climb the moor to the Pipers Crag to look out over the whole twenty seven acres with the valley beyond. Joanna puts her firm hand into mine to come and feed the hens and collect the eggs. I hear all the news of school and home.

WHAT HAPPENED TO THEM ALL ...

Aunt Anna, my father's sister, was buried in the Quaker grave-yard at Jordons, one of the very early Quaker Meeting Houses. The last of her generation, she had written to Rigmor saying 'I am last, I am alone'. They had a very strong friendship up until her death.

Rigmor had been greatly influenced by her time spent at the Quaker Woodbrooke College, while living at my Dad's house, South Hill. Every letter Rigmor sent to me had some reference or reflection upon her time there. As she grew older some of her twice yearly communications, one at Christmas and one at around 10th April my Dad's birthday would contain a book she had been given at South Hill or a tray cloth which she had worked when young or photographs . . .

After the war she had taught handicapped children and in later life she married a teacher, Hans. They lived contentedly in a love-ly house in Jutland, Denmark. Her brother had gone to South Africa and he had been killed during the uprisings against apartheid. Like Ringmor when her family had hidden a Jewish girl in their attic throughout the war, her brother had stood up for the right ideals.

Rigmor wrote in her near faultless English this to me in 1978 ...

> 'I live in a world among the present and future gener-ations as well as among those gone before us. Recently I dreamt I walked along a shore line with my brother who died in 1970. Suddenly I looked at him in the strange-familiar surroundings and asked him 'But where are we?' and he answered 'in the same world of God, with a small stream parting us'. I awoke with a smile and with a comforted feeling. He is ahead of me in a fairer world.'

I had a dream after my sister's death. It was not betwixt heaven and earth. It was fun, and a little sad. We seemed to be about

132

eight years old — I wrote it down like this

> Al
> I went to bed aching and tired
> When Al ran in and jumped on my bed
> 'If you're real touch my toes'
> I cried as I stood
> Blue eyed, and laughing.
> She tapped on my foot
> I looked down where she'd lain
> hair flung back from her head
> But as was our youth
> Alice had gone.

Rigmor's last letter came at Christmas 1990. Her eyesight was failing, her handwriting had deteriorated and her rheumatism was severe. It had been a very long time since she had shown us how to do handstands in the sitting room at Chantersleur. I think she must have crossed 'her small stream' by now.

My Uncle Wilfrid (my Dad's nephew) and Aunt Winifred moved to an old people's bungalow opposite our house South Hill. Whether the road had been widened, my Dad's great fear, while they lived there I do not know. Later they went to live at Jordans with my cousin Margaret. Her husband Kevin had died and their son and three daughters were all grown up. Wilfrid and Winifred died in their nineties. Up until the end they kept up their Quaker way of speech, 'thee' and 'thou' when addressing each other. With their quiet voices they must have been amongst the very last in the country to speak in this pleasant sounding way.

Hugh, Mollie, Janet and Kay of Chantersleur and Hill Farm ... When the estate in Somerset had to be sold up Hugh and Mollie had to leave Hill Farm for a job in Berkhampstead, Hertfordshire. They moved to a roomy semi-detached house, and began to make a new garden. Janet was encouraged to go to Australia. Mollie liked England, she loved the rain and the crisp frosty mornings, but she missed the beaches. There the sun shone, she told us, and the great white topped waves rolled in on to silver sand. She wanted her daughter to meet Mr Williams, her brother in law from Wales, and her other relations. Janet got a job as a cook on a sheep station in the outback. She still could enjoy her love of horses and riding. Eventually she married a fellow worker. They had no children of their own but adopted twin boys. Soon afterwards Janet's husband died and she later married again. They devoted themselves to their boys who sadly had to have special schooling and eventually worked and lived in sheltered housing, spending free time and holidays with Janet and Max. From their big windowed house, set in rolling bush country, Janet did a full time job in the Council Buildings at Nambour, Queensland.

When Hugh died, Mollie decided to return to Australia and live near Janet. She packed up all her things and most of the lovely antique furniture collected over the years, and shipped it out to Nambour. After some months she found she could not settle, so leaving the furniture with Janet, she returned to live in one of two country cottages outside Berkhampstead. By now Kay had two young boys under six and his wife had unfortunately died. Eventually Kay was able to move in next door to Mollie and with her cheerful ways and her superb knack of looking after other people's children, she helped bring them up into their teens. In her eighties, in her little bedroom with the sloping polished floor and the white cottage ceiling under the eaves, Mollie died in the night. She had been planning to decorate the sitting room next day!

Uncle Roland had a few happy years of retirement at Lastingham. After he died Aunt Grace went to live in Glossop with Nan and her husband Joe, living until her mid eighties. Nan and Joe were teachers and brought up their three boys in Glossop After retirement, Nan started work raising money for 'The Winged Fellowship', an organisation who plan suitable holiday activities for disabled people. She has done and is still doing a most marvellous and energetic job.

After a career in medicine, Bill and his wife Mary, (who lived in

Wales, Jamaica and London during their working lives) moved to a large house in a quiet corner of the Lake District near Staveley to live with Nan and Joe. They divided the house into two and with their family of four sons and a daughter and Nan's three boys and all their grandchildren they have huge family gatherings interspaced with their hobbies and interests.

When I last visited Nan, our visits have not been frequent, although always pleasant! Bill called me into his sitting room to show me a small wooden box. It had, he said, been intricately carved by a fellow prisoner of war, and had been sent home to his father my Uncle Roland near the end of the war. On its journey to this country it had nearly been smashed. 'My father', Bill said 'almost completed its destruction by trying to mend it with nails'. The box had been removed from storage to be the subject of a painting entitled 'A Treasured Possession' — both he and Mary had become talented painters in their retirement. As Bill held the box out towards me his hand shook slightly. I drew my hand back as I was about to take the box from him to look more closely. I knew instinctively that this was one possession Bill would never wish to hand over to anyone else to hold. I felt honoured to be shown it.

Last November I heard from Nan that Leonard would be 80 next birthday. We had not been in the habit of sending cards except at Christmas. I thought hard... what was the date of his birthday? Eventually I picked the wrong one — Bill's. This led to a very pleasant conversation on the telephone with Leonard. His three sons and a daughter were all doing well. He was to visit one son s a broadcaster on Australian Television — for Christmas. the son had recently produced a delightful film called 'Strictly Ballroom' for Australian viewing which later earned an award at the Cannes Film Festival. A riotous film of music and dance, I was advised to see it — which I did, and found it a pleasure to watch When my birthday came round again the telephone rang and it was Leonard. He had returned safely and was ringing to wish me a happy birthday. 'Three score years and ten' he said 'you have had your allotted span, now every year is a bonus'.

When I put the phone down I thought 'Yes, that is it, that is my title for the story'. I had been wandering about the fields watching the spring unfold once again, with my dog Bess beside me, trying to think of a title. Three score years and ten, and now I am to start on my bonus.

And what of Mary and Jim ... We have the bonus of still being together, and of being able to watch our grandchildren grow up in a very different world. In this story I have tried to explain some of the ideals which the people around me had and passed on to me. In gratefulness to them all, I try to pass on again a tiny measure of the same to my grandchildren.